KU-073-235

The best of
FLORENCE

CAROLINE KOUBÉ

GLOBETROTTER™

First edition published in 2002
by New Holland Publishers (UK) Ltd
London • Cape Town • Sydney • Auckland
10 9 8 7 6 5 4 3 2 1

website: www.newhollandpublishers.com

Garfield House, 86 Edgware Road
London W2 2EA
United Kingdom

80 McKenzie Street
Cape Town 8001
South Africa

14 Aquatic Drive
Frenchs Forest, NSW 2086
Australia

218 Lake Road
Northcote, Auckland
New Zealand

Distributed in the USA by
The Globe Pequot Press, Connecticut

Copyright © 2002 in text: Caroline Koubé
Copyright © 2002 in maps: Globetrotter
Travel Maps
Copyright © 2002 in photographs:
Individual photographers as credited (right)
Copyright © 2002 New Holland Publishers
(UK) Ltd

ISBN 1 84330 291 8

Publishing Manager (UK): Simon Pooley
Publishing Manager (SA): John Loubser
Managing Editor: Thea Grobbelaar
DTP Cartographic Manager: Genené Hart
Editor: Jacqueline de Villiers

Designer: Lellyn Creamer
Cover Design: Lellyn Creamer, Nicole Engeler
Cartographer: Genené Hart
Proofreader: Nicole Engeler

Reproduction by Resolution (Cape Town) and
Hirt & Carter (Pty) Ltd, Cape Town
Printed and bound in Hong Kong by Sing Cheong
Printing Co. Ltd.

Although every effort has been made to ensure
that this guide is up to date and current at time
of going to print, the Publisher accepts no
responsibility or liability for any loss, injury or
inconvenience incurred by readers or travellers
using this guide.

Acknowledgments:
The author would like to thank the following
people and organizations for their generous
assistance: the staff of the APT offices in
Arezzo, Pisa and Siena, Judi Chatfield
Schwerin, Sara Louise Harper and Enzo
Manzoni.

Photographic Credits:
AA Travel Library: page 54;
Mark Azavedo: page 63;
Paul Bernhardt: pages 16, 18, 24;
Bridgeman Art Library: page 22;
Empics Sport Photo Agency: page 73;
The Hutchison Library/John Hatt: page 20;
Image-Link: title page, pages 6, 8, 9, 10, 12,
13, 17, 19, 21, 23, 25, 26, 27, 28, 29, 30, 31,
32, 34, 35, 36, 37, 39, 40, 41, 42, 43, 45, 46,
47, 48, 53, 60, 61, 65, 71, 74, 75, 76, 77, 78,
79, 82, 83;
Life File/Giles Stokoe: page 62;
Life File/Andrew Ward: pages 11, 44;
Richard Sale: front cover, pages 7, 14, 15, 33,
50, 81;
Struik Image Library/Craig Fraser: page 66;
Gregory Wrona: page 84.

Front Cover: *Ponte Vecchio, Florence's oldest
bridge, spans the River Arno.*
Title Page: *Fra Angelico's Madonna, Child and
Saints, San Marco.*

CONTENTS

MAKE THE MOST OF YOUR GUIDE

Reading these two pages will help you to get the most out of your guide and save you time when using it. Sites discussed in the text are cross-referenced with the cover maps – for example, the reference 'Map B–C3' refers to the Greater Florence Map (Map B), column C, row 3. Use the Map Plan below to quickly locate the map you need.

MAP PLAN

Outside Back Cover

Outside Front Cover

Inside Front Cover

Inside Back Cover

THE BIGGER PICTURE

Key to Map Plan

A – Excursions Map
B – Greater Florence
C – Central Florence
D – Siena
E – Pisa
F – Galleria degli Uffizi
G – Galleria Palatina

Key to Symbols

⊠ – address

☎ – telephone

✆ – fax

🖳 – website

✍️ – e-mail address

🕐 – opening times

🚌 – tour

💰 – entry fee

🍴 – restaurants nearby

Map Legend

motorway	═══	main road	**Via G. Verdi**
national road	═══	pedestrian mall	VIA DEL CORSO
main road	═══	other road	Via di Mezzo
minor road	═══	wall	▬▬▬
railway	────	built-up area	
ferry	─ ─ ─	market	Mercato Centrale
river	～ Arno	hotel	(H) DALÍ
route number	☐1	building of interest	Teatro Verdi
city	**FLORENCE (FIRENZE)**	library	📖
major town	🏛 **Arezzo**	place of interest	• Museo Marino Marini
town	○ San Miniato	post office	⊠
large village	◎ Certaldo	parking area	🅿
village	○ Meleto	tourist information	🛈
airport	✈ ✈	place of worship	△ Santa Trinità
peaks in metres	M. la Faggeta ▲ 1144 m	police station	●
cave	⦿ Grotta d. Vento	bus terminus	🚍
ruin	∴ Castel Vecchio	hospital	⊕
safe bathing	≈	park & garden	Giardino di Boboli
beach	⌣		

Keep us Current

Travel information is apt to change, which is why we regularly update our guides. We'd be most grateful to receive feedback from you if you've noted something we should include in our updates. If you have any new information, please share it with us by writing to the Publishing Manager, Globetrotter, at the office nearest to you (addresses on the imprint page of this guide). The most significant contribution to each new edition will be rewarded with a free copy of the updated guide.

Above: *Sunflowers colour the Tuscan hills in summer.*

OVERVIEW

Florence is the grand old lady of Italy. Sophisticated, cultured, wise and redolent in magnificent history, this Tuscan city did as much to shape European civilization as Rome did some 1800 years earlier. Straddling the River Arno it is a city surrounded by the beautiful hills of Tuscany, likewise known for their delightful Medieval and Renaissance villages and towns. Thanks to the rise in mercantile wealth during the 14th century, Florence's elite prospered and gave back to their city astonishing churches, palaces and paintings. Florence today, is simply the most elegant of Italian towns.

The Land
Climate

Tuscany bathes in a Mediterranean climate which, in Florence, is slightly cooler in winter, and hotter in summer. Rainfall is higher in spring and autumn – probably the most comfortable time to explore the city.

Plant Life

Florentines escape to the perennially green hills of Tuscany as the city has little to offer. However, most visitors and many locals spend time in the splendid Giardino di Boboli, the Boboli Garden just behind Palazzo Pitti, and stroll along the banks of the Arno.

Wildlife

Florence is not the best spot for wildlife. However, visitors who explore the surrounding countryside will find fields full of wildflowers in spring, fabulous forests on the upper slopes of the Appenine Mountains and see the occasional migratory bird.

<u>Climate</u>
Winter is generally cool at 8–14°C (46–57°C) with slightly more rainfall in November and December. **Spring** can be rainy, but will also be sunny. **Summer**, from June to early September, is warm, peaking at around 30°C (86°F) in the hot summer afternoons, and rainfall is rarely more than a short and sharp thunder shower. **Autumn** is a very pleasant time – the days are shorter, temperatures are lower, but the weather is often dry.

History in Brief

Documented history in Tuscany starts with the **Etruscans** who flourished around 800BC in the coastal regions of modern Tuscany and Lazio, establishing agriculture, far-reaching trading links and a thriving economy based on mineral wealth and metals. Tuscany is littered with the remains of Etruscan villages, statuary and tombs.

Under the Romans

Over the following centuries, through warfare and cultural absorption, Etruria gradually became part of the **Roman Republic** (later Empire). The Romans built roads such as the Via Cassia and Via Aurelia and colonized enthusiastically, often on Etruscan sites, to consolidate their rule. **Florence** was founded by Julius Caesar as the easiest point to cross the Arno and settled by army veterans.

Christianity reached Tuscany in the early 2nd century. Meanwhile, the Roman Empire declined and fell and it was divided into East and West. The Western Empire became prey to **Goths** and **Vandals**, barbarian forces from northern Europe, and in 476 the king of the Goths, **Odoacar**, deposed Emperor Romulus Augustulus, ending the Western Empire.

With the rise of the city states in Tuscany, Florence became a self-governing commune in the 12th century and began its slow, but certain, domination of the whole region. Internal strife, however, destroyed much

> **Etruscan Soothsayers**
> To the Etruscans, death was terrifying, and they longed for reassurance about the future. As a result, the Etruscans specialized in divination: they examined animals' entrails, the flight of birds and bolts of lightning. Every legion of the Roman army had an Etruscan soothsayer and when the state fell on evil days, the soothsayers were summoned to Rome and their ceremonies revived and faithfully observed under the Romans.

Below: *The Roman theatre at Fiesole, near Florence, is one of Tuscany's best preserved.*

Guelf or Ghibelline?
The name '**Guelf**' originates from the Welf family, who supported the papacy. In Florence the Guelfs were then further divided into the Neri (Blacks) and Bianchi (Whites). Florentine families took opposite sides and the quarrel led to the exile of Dante from Florence in 1302 when the city was purged of the Whites. '**Ghibelline**' may originate from Waiblingen, the name of an estate belonging to the Holy Roman Emperors, or from their battle cry of 'Hie Weibling'.

of the social fabric of each Tuscan town as inhabitants sided either with the papal Guelfs or the imperial Ghibellines yet Florence continued to prosper.

The Renaissance

Banking, money-lending and the wool trade were responsible for Florence's 14th and 15th century prosperity. The increasingly powerful guilds and families with or without noble blood began to divert some of their riches and created fabulous family **chapels, churches, hospitals,** and huge **palaces** all decorated with impressive works of sculpture and painting. Thus the Italian Renaissance gradually took form and artisans were to enjoy an unprecedented period of work. The guilds prospered, competition for contracts was fierce, and the standards of architecture, painting, stonework and sculpture rose in leaps and bounds.

Among the families who rose to positions of prominence, were the Medici. **Cosimo de Medici** returned from exile in 1434 and the family were to play an important behind-the-scenes role in Florence. It was his more famous grandson, **Lorenzo il Magnifico,** who did the most to make the family name. A man interested in the arts, his patronage and that of his contemporaries contributed to the commissioning of some of Europe's greatest works.

In 1494, Charles VII of France invaded Italy and the golden age started to fragment. Cosimo I became Grand Duke and the Medicis remained in prominence for another two centuries.

Below: *Cosimo de Medici surveys the elegant buildings in Piazza Santa Trinità.*

Unification

By the mid 1800s, political unrest swept through the Italian peninsula and the ultimate failure of the 1848 revolutions proved that the expulsion of foreigners required consummate diplomatic and military skills. These talents were provided by the diplomat, **Count Camillo di Cavour**, and the

soldier, **Giuseppe Garibaldi**. Between them they finally achieved the unification of Italy in 1861. Florence was capital until 1871, when Rome became the capital of a united Italy.

Above: *Freedom fighter Giuseppe Garibaldi meets King Vittorio Emanuele II.*

The Twentieth Century

Florence suffered during World War II when Mussolini took Italy to war. All the bridges, except the Ponte Vecchio, were blown up by the Germans, and in 1944 the city was occupied by the Allies. In 1966 the River Arno rose to unprecedented heights and flooded some parts of the city, including the Uffizi Gallery. Now largely restored, Florence has rediscovered a new elegance.

Government and Economy

Tuscany is ruled from Rome. However, for economic and cultural purposes the region bands together, lead by the most important province, Florence. Five hundred years ago cloth, banking, stone and agriculture were mainstays of the economy. Today, the economy is kept afloat by tourism (over seven million tourists visit Florence annually), fashion and light industry. The industrial areas are to be found in Florence's satellite towns such as Sesto Fiorentino and Scandicci, urban areas which have now become indistinguishable from the larger city's own suburbs.

> **Michelangelo Buonarroti (1475–1564)**
> Michelangelo was born in Caprese but grew up in Florence. At 13 years old he was apprenticed to painter Domenico Ghirlandaio. His first major works – the **Bacchus** in Florence's Bargello and the **Pietà** in St Peter's, Rome – show a gentle sculptor, not yet fascinated by the muscular body of later years. He returned to Florence in 1501 and produced **David** in the Accademia and the lovely **Doni Tondo** in the Uffizi. In 1520, after completing the **Sistine Chapel in Rome**, he started the sculpture for the **Medici Chapel**.

The People

Language

Italian is the lingua franca of Italy and, it is said, at its purest in Florence. The Florentines have their own dialect – but to the passing tourist, it will probably all sound much the same. Thanks to centuries of diplomatic exchange, and now television and the Internet, the urban Tuscans have picked up foreign languages. For the tourist whose vocabulary is limited to a simple *buon giorno, grazie* and *ciao*, there will be little problem in communication, for the Tuscans will want to practice their language skills.

Above: *Piazza della Repubblica's sunny outdoor terrace is a popular gathering point for Florentine society.*

Religion

Roman Catholicism has always had a strong foothold in Tuscany and as you wander through the region's myriad churches and cathedrals, the various orders will start to distinguish themselves. Benedictine, Cicstercian, Dominican, Franciscan, Carthusian and Carmelites form the backbone of the religious community.

Although the Catholic clergy has reduced in number over the centuries, and the Church in influence, they are still present but gather smaller congregations (and fewer wealthy patrons). Many churches are having difficulty in making ends meet and in some places not only are they open for just a short period daily but there may be an entrance fee to see artistic treasures.

Famous Foreigners in Florence
Lured by its cultural environment, a number of **English** and **American writers** chose to visit or to live for long periods in Florence. These include:
Bernard Berenson, art historian;
EM Forster, author of *A Room with a View*, set in Florence;
DH Lawrence;
Elizabeth Barrett Browning;
Henry James, author of *The Portrait of a Lady*, set in Florence

---

For the sizeable non-Catholic population there are also Protestant churches and a well-patronized synagogue in Florence.

The Arts
From those early days of the Etruscans and Romans, little exists in Florence itself. The arts began to flourish from the late **Middle Ages**, and with an increase in mercantile wealth, another wave of religious construction took form. The local guilds were particularly strong and undertook many new building projects. Interestingly, Florence was little influenced by her neighbours or trading partners, and moved art into a new era.

By the late 13th century, Ancient Rome had been rediscovered. Artists were ripe for a new realism, a three-dimensionality, a simplification of style and even new subject matter – religious works had been, until this time, the norm.

Giotto (1266–1337) was the first artist to be accorded a new type of status. A master of fresco painting who looked at traditional scenes with new eyes, he was charged with overseeing the rebuilding of Florence's **Duomo**. He was chosen not for his architectural record, but because he was a fine forward-thinking painter, with a reputation in the arts.

By the 1400s, the new nobles of Florence (led by the powerful Medici family) saw the many advantages of patronage and began sponsoring the building of chapels and charitable foundations. Such commissions ushered in the great flowering of art known as the **Renaissance**.

Learning the Lingo
Tuscany has long been a favourite place to study Italian. Thanks to Dante, it was the birthplace of modern Italian, and in addition, the historical environment is so conducive and the language schools are excellent.
Dante Alighieri School for Foreigners,
✉ via dei Bardi 12,
☎ 055 23429986.
Istituto di Lingua e Cultura Italiana per Stranieri,
✉ via Ghibellina 88,
☎ 055 240975.
British Institute,
✉ piazza Strozzi 2,
☎ 055 284033.

Below: *One of the sculptured alcoves on Florence's Duomo.*

OVERVIEW

Leonardo da Vinci (1452–1519)

Leonardo, one of the creators of the High Renaissance, was born in 1452. He trained as a painter under Verocchio and by the late 1470s had a fine reputation. His first existing masterpiece, the unfinished *Adoration of the Magi* (1481, Uffizi) shows his talents for observation. He went to Milan in 1483 and painted the *Last Supper* in 1497. In 1500 he studied anatomy in Florence, started *Madonna and Child with St Anne* and completed the *Mona Lisa*. Appointed Engineer and Painter to Louis XII in 1507, he moved to France where he died in 1519.

Below: *A fine statue portraying the great Leonardo da Vinci, outside the Uffizi.*

In **architecture** an early innovator was **Brunelleschi** (1377–1446). He started out as a goldsmith and sculptor but turned his hand to architecture, having studied perspective and Roman buildings, and became one of the founding fathers of the Renaissance. In his wake, **Michelozzo** (1396–1472) became Cosimo the Elder's favourite architect, while Giuliano **da Sangallo** (1443–1516) and the great **Michelangelo** (1475–1564) were to continue the trend for later Medicis. **Leon Battista Alberti** (1404–72) studied classical remains in Rome, wrote a treatise on architecture and tried to adapt Roman civic architecture to religious and domestic uses.

The Baptistry of St John (*see* page 17) contains some of Florence's greatest **sculpture**, from the South Doors created by **Andrea Pisano** (ca. 1270–1349) to the North and East Doors created by **Lorenzo Ghiberti** (1378–1455). **Donatello** (ca. 1385–1466) introduced a new force and realism into sculpture, for instance in his famous bronze *David*. He influenced much of later Florentine sculpture and was unmatched until **Michelangelo** arrived. Michelangelo's giant *David* (*see* page 24), commissioned for Florence's Piazza della Signoria, is the most famous of all Renaissance sculptures.

In **painting**, it was **Masaccio** (1401–28) who led the way to the Renaissance (*see* panel, page 15). When he frescoed part of the Brancacci Chapel and created Santa Maria Novella's *Holy Trinity with Virgin, St John and Donors*, painting took another great leap forward.

Following in Masaccio's footsteps (according to chronicler Vasari, everyone studied his work) came the less innovative but popular **Paolo Uccello** (ca. 1396–1475) whose subjects showed his preoccupation with perspective (see page 14). The great masters of fresco include **Fra Angelico** (1400–55), who grasped the concept of perspective, but clung to soft, gentle colours and images to convey a certain purity of spirit; the talented **Fra Filippo Lippi** (1406–69); and his son, **Filippino** (ca. 1457–1504). Filippo taught **Sandro Botticelli** (1445–1510), who rose to be one of the great individuals in the Renaissance (many of his works are displayed in the Uffizi, including his famous painting *The Birth of Venus*).

In the mid-15th century other notable artists were in great demand. These included **Piero della Francesca** (1416–92), **Luca Signorelli** (ca. 1441–1523) and **Perugino** (1446–1523). The works of the brilliant polymath **Leonardo da Vinci** (1452–1519, *see panel, page 12*) ushered in the High Renaissance. Famous for his paintings and scientific drawings, da Vinci's *Mona Lisa* is probably the world's best known painting.

Raffaello Sanzio (**Raphael**, 1483–1520) was one of the greats of the High Renaissance. His *La Velata* and other works are on display in the Pitti Palace. **Michelangelo**, a great sculptor, was an equally brilliant painter. His famous *Pietà* is in the Museo dell'Opera del Duomo.

Literature

Three of Italy's finest writers – Boccaccio, Dante and Petrarch – were born at a time when most writing was in Latin. Then **Dante** (*see panel, page 42*) began a movement to write in the vernacular. His famous allegorical poem, *Divine Comedy*, still makes good reading. So too does **Boccaccio's** *Decameron*. The earthiness of Boccaccio's work contrasts with the elegance of that of **Petrarch**, one of Italy's greatest poets. Another famous name is **Niccolò Machiavelli**, author of *The Prince*.

Above: *This copy of Michelangelo's* David *now stands in for the original on the Piazza della Signoria.*

The Guild System

The guilds were originally formed to protect the interests of Florence's commercial classes. The council of Florence was formed of members elected from the city's guilds, appointed for a fixed term, but some guilds were much more influential than others. For a long time the power of the guilds enabled Florence to avoid despotism and remain a republic, but it was far from democratic. In 1378 the *Ciompi*, the lowest paid of the wool workers, rebelled, demanding the right to form their own guild and be represented on the council. After initial victory the movement failed for lack of support among the humbler guilds.

Galleria degli Uffizi
🕐 08:15–18:50 Tue–
Fri, 08:15–22:00 Sat,
08:30–19:00 Sun;
closed Mon
✉ Palazzo degli
Uffizi, piazzale degli
Uffizi 6
☎ 055 2388616 or
294883 for advance
bookings; otherwise
be prepared to queue
🖰 info@www.uffizi.
firenze.it
🖥 www.uffizi.firenze.it
🖥 www.sbas.firenze.
it/uffizi/
🍴 There is a cafeteria
on the third floor.

See Map F   ★ ★ ★

GALLERIA DEGLI UFFIZI

Within this large and impressive art gallery (best visited in the late afternoon when it is less crowded) there are some fabulous paintings, many of which will be familiar from reproductions. Mentioned below are a few that merit closer appreciation.

Room 2 houses some early 13th-century works which set the scene for understanding painting at the end of the Middle Ages. There are three interpretations of the *Maestà* by the early masters – **Cimabue**, **Duccio**, and the later painter, **Giotto**.

Room 7 opens onto some familiar sights. A magnificent rendering of the *Virgin and Child with St Anne* by the Gothic painter **Masolino** and his young associate, **Masaccio** (*see* panel, page 15). It shows Masaccio's ability to grasp the concepts of the role light plays in modelling form and dimension. There is also the marvellous profile portrait of *Federico de Montefeltro and Battista Sforza*, the Dukes of Monte-feltro, painted in 1472 by **Piero della Francesca**. The delicate landscapes in the background owe their style more, perhaps, to the Flemish school of painting than the Italian. Nearby is the one large panel from the triptych, *The Battle of San Romano* by **Paolo Uccello**, painted in the mid-15th century for Cosimo the Elder.

It is an action-packed battle scene (look how Uccello has created three-dimensional if

Opposite: *A detail from Botticelli's* Allegory of Spring. **Below:** *Part of Michelangelo's famous painting,* The Holy Family.

rather wooden subjects, and how he has mastered foreshortening in the fallen soldier) depicting the Florentine victory over the Sienese in 1432.

Room 8 contains works by Filippo Lippi (1406–69), ex-Carmelite monk turned painter who learned from Masaccio and who, in turn, taught his son, Filippino, and Botticelli. His *Virgin and Child with two Saints*, painted in 1464, reflects the sensual nature of this talented painter.

Rooms 10–14, now forming one gallery, are devoted to works by **Sandro Botticelli**. His two famous works, The *Allegory of Spring* and *The Birth of Venus*, are both infinitely more impressive when you stand in front of them than their oft-seen reproductions. The delicacy of brushwork and the fragility of human beauty is captured in a novel way, confirming Botticelli's talent.

Room 15 displays work by **Leonardo da Vinci**, and includes his very early but quite beautiful *Annunciation* (still influenced by his teacher, Verrocchio) and the unfinished 1481 masterpiece, *Adoration of the Magi*, an illustration of many of the Renaissance's principles of design and form.

Room 25 houses **Michelangelo**'s beautiful tondo (round painting) of *The Holy Family*, painted for the Doni family in 1504. It was one of his last Florentine commissions before he started work on the Sistine Chapel in Rome.

Room 26 displays, among other fine paintings, **Andrea del Sarto**'s powerful 1517 *Madonna of the Harpies*.

Room 28 is home to the gallery's collection of **Titian**'s canvases such as the famous reclining *Venus of Urbino*.

Masaccio
Born 1401 at the peak of Gothic Art and dead aged 27, it is Tommaso di Giovanni di Simone Guidi, nicknamed **Masaccio**, Big Tom, who is credited with changing the face of Florentine painting through his lifelike and emotional work in the Brancacci Chapel. With his elder, intellectual and humanist friends, **Brunelleschi** and **Donatello**, they formed the talented triumvirate which moved art into the Renaissance. Quoting chronocler **Vasari**: *'There are still some heads to be seen there which are so beautiful and lifelike that one can say outright that no other painter of that time approached the modern style of painting as closely as did Masaccio.'* Raphael, Michelangelo and Leonardo da Vinci all studied his frescoes in the chapel.

Above: *The Duomo's cupola is a familiar Florentine landmark.*

Duomo and Cupola
🕐 10:00–17:00 daily,
13:00–17:00 public
holidays (Duomo);
08:30–19:00 Mon–Fri,
18:30–17:40 Sat,
closed Sun and holi-
days (cupola)
✉ Piazza del Duomo
☎ 055 2302885
(cupola)
💻 www.mega.it/eng/
egui/monu/buq.htm
💰 Duomo free of
charge; entry fee to
visit the cupola
🍽 restaurants nearby

See Map C–E3   ★★★

DUOMO

The exterior of this imposing cathedral, dedicated to **Santa Maria del Fiore**, is beautiful (the interior, by contrast, is rather plain) but its cupola is magnificent. It is one of Christendom's largest cathedrals, as befitted the rising economic and cultural wealth of Medieval Florence, and is capped by a spectacular dome with an equally spectacular view once the 460-odd wearing steps have been climbed. Towering above the neighbouring palaces, the dome of this substantial building provides a guiding landmark for pedestrians. It was **Arnolfo di Cambio** (ca. 1245–1302) who accepted the prestigious commission and it is his Gothic design we see today, though the red-roofed dome, designed in 1433 to cover the huge sanctuary, was the work of ground-breaking architect **Brunelleschi** (*see page 12*). He conceived his sectioned dome much like an egg, with a smaller inner layer and a solid outer layer, with supports between the two. Between these architects, painter **Giotto** (*see page 11*) was nominated Master of Works by the Medici family, who sought to have a 'famous name' in charge, rather than a trained but unknown overseer. The west façade, originally designed by di Cambio, was reclad in the now familiar green, russet and white marbles during the 19th century.

See Map C–D3   ★★★

Battistero
🕐 12:00–19:00
Mon–Sat, 08:30–14:00
Sun and holidays
✉ Piazza di San Giovanni
☎ 055 2302885
🖥 www.arca.net.db/musei/baptist.htm
💰 entry fee
🍴 restaurants nearby

BATTISTERO

Marvellous as the Medieval, octagonal Baptistry of St John may be, it's the doors which draw the crowds. A competition for two pairs of new bronze doors was launched in 1401 (Andrea Pisano had executed the first pair in 1330) and anybody who was notable in the art world clamoured to submit designs. It was young sculptor **Lorenzo Ghiberti** (1378–1455) who won the commission and his North Doors, harmonizing well with Pisano's work, show scenes from the Life of Christ, the Evangelists and the Doctors of the Church (with a self-portrait on the frame). But it's the **East Doors**, the 10 panels of the so-called **Gates of Paradise** (Michelangelo is said to have dubbed them thus) which are truly superb (the originals are in the Museo dell'Opera del Duomo). Old Testament scenes unfold with realism and poetry. Save time to admire the glittering *trecento* (see panel, page 21) mosaics inside, among which are scenes fashioned by the best of Venetian craftsmen taken from both Testaments.

If you haven't climbed to the top of the Duomo, the view from the **Campanile** (the bell tower) is similar. Designed by Giotto in 1334 and clad in coloured marbles, the belfry is probably the most elegant Gothic landmark in Florence.

Below: *Intricate marble work decorates the Baptistery, Belfry and the Duomo.*

Piazza della Signoria
🖥 www.arca.net.db/
musei/pvecchio.htm
🍽 There are many
restaurants and cafés
nearby.

See Map C–E4   ★★★

PIAZZA DELLA SIGNORIA

Erstwhile centre of civic activity, site of Savonarola's 1498 death by burning, Piazza della Signoria is still the political centre of Florence and a meeting place for tourists and Florentines alike. It is dominated by the superb **Palazzo Vecchio**, flanked by the **Loggia della Signoria**, (the **Uffizi Gallery** is just behind) and rimmed by other palaces. In the centre stands the equestrian sculpture of **Cosimo I**, a 1594 work by Giovanni da Bologna (also known as Giambologna). The piazza is now dressed with smart *caffès*, perfect for people watching. Other decorative items in this large square (this a place also to pick up a horse-drawn cab to visit the pedestrian centre of town) are a rather streaky copy of Michelangelo's sculpture, *Davide* (David in English; now situated in the Galleria dell'Accademia) which was originally commissioned for this piazza, and the impressive **Neptune Fountain**, work of Bartolomeo Ammannati.

Below: *The statue of Neptune (nick-named Il Biancone, the Fat White One) provides the centrepiece for Ammannati's* Neptune Fountain, *created in 1656.*

🕐 *See* Map C–E5   ★ ★ ★

PALAZZO VECCHIO

Likewise known by its original name (Palazzo della Signoria), this was the seat of local government, a solid town hall with an elegant tower, probably another work by the cathedral's architect, Arnolfo di Cambio. Medici favourite Michelozzo was commissioned to redesign parts of the palace in the *quattrocento*, while in the 16th century Cosimo I appropriated it as his residence and called upon his architect, Vasari, to renovate and decorate it to accommodate his luxurious lifestyle.

Above *Medieval masterpiece, the Palazzo Vecchio.*

The Palazzo (open daily) can be visited. Highlights include Vasari's delicate courtyard, the magnificent and cavernous Hall of the 500 decorated by Vasari, the rather claustrophobic but elegant Studiolo, once the study of Francesco I (another superb Vasari work), and the extensive apartments on the third floor.

Adjacent to the Palazzo, another major feature of the Piazza della Signoria is the famous **Loggia della Signoria**.

The fashion for loggias began at the turn of the 13th century. This Gothic one, with its rounded arches, was constucted to shelter civil servants during official ceremonies in the piazza. Sometimes called the **Loggia dei Lanzi**, it shelters some exquisite sculpture such as the slightly disturbing *Perseus* (1545) holding up Medusa's severed head, by *cinquecento* goldsmith and sculptor, **Benvenuto Cellini** and the powerful *Rape of the Sabines* (1583) by **Giambologna**.

Palazzo Vecchio
🕐 09:00–19:00 Fri–Wed, 09:00–14:00 Thu in winter; 09:00–19:00 Tue, Wed, Sat, 09:00–23:00 Mon and Fri, and 09:00–14:00 Thu in summer
✉ Piazza della Signoria
☎ 055 2768465
✆ sat@commune.firenze.it
🖥 www.arca.net.db/musei/pvecchio.htm
🖥 www.commune.fi.it/servizi_pubblici/arte/musei/a.htm
🍽 restaurants and cafés in the piazza

HIGHLIGHTS

Above: *The mournful gaze of Niccolò da Uzzano, a sculpture attributed to Donatello.*
Opposite: *Built over 800 years ago, and surviving civil war and World War II, the Ponte Vecchio links Renaissance and Medieval Florence.*

See Map C–F4 ★★★

PALAZZO DEL BARGELLO

Severe and uninviting, this Medieval palace houses the **Museo del Bargello**, which contains a fine collection of sculpture and decorative arts. The building was begun in 1250, when it was crowned with its crenellated tower and grew through the following century, and has successively housed political figures, police and prisoners.

Among the most impressive works of art in this museum are the early works by **Michelangelo** (his rather unappealing *Drunk Bacchus*), the *Tondo Pitti*, a round three-dimensional sculpture, destined to be hung on the wall, depicting the Virgin, child and St John. Don't overlook the Bust of *Cosimo I* (and other works) by **Benvenuto Cellini**, the master goldsmith, sculptor and writer. The works by **Donatello** merit close appreciation. Look at his classical bronze *David*, the first bronze of a nude statue since Classical times, and compare it with his much earlier, marble version. Don't miss the *Madonna and Child* by another great and innovative sculptor, **Luca della Robbia**. This master of glazed terracotta produced many delightful semi-three-dimensional sculptures in white, usually on a blue background. The work of **Verrocchio**, another leading Renaissance sculptor, is represented by, among others, his *David*. Save some time for the exhibits of carpets and arms in the **Sala Islamica**, the ivories in the **Sala delgi Avori** and the items on display in the Sala Carrand, a varied collection of artifacts bequeathed to Florence by Frenchman Louis Carrand.

Palazzo del Bargello
🕐 08:15–13:50
Tue–Sat, 08:15–17:00
Sun, closed Mon.
✉ Via del Proconsolo 4
☎ 055 2388606
☎ 055 294883 for advance bookings
✆ segretaria@ sbas.firenze.it
🖥 www.sbas.firenze.it/ bargello/index.html
🖥 www.arca.net.db/ musei/bargello.htm
💰 entry fee
🍴 in Piazza della Signoria or Piazza del Duomo.

See Map C–D5 | ★★★

PONTE VECCHIO

Since Roman times, this strategic point between the north and south banks of the Arno has been linked by a bridge. It is the narrowest part of the river and links the heart of Florence and the Oltrarno. This landmark bridge (the 'Old Bridge') has twice been lashed by the churning waters of the flooding Arno. The 1170 bridge was washed away in 1333 and rebuilt in 1345 when butchers and tanners occupied its various shops, making use of the Arno for their waste. So great was the resulting stench that Grand Duke Ferdinando I evicted them at the end of the 14th century and let the space to jewellers and silversmiths. In the 17th century their workshops were enlarged by cantilevering the floors outwards on wooden poles. During World War II the Ponte Vecchio was the only bridge to be spared in the 1944 raid.

On 4 November 1966, the Arno rose once more and the bridge was yet again under threat. Although quite some damage was done it was fortunately not irreparable.

The old jewellery tradition still continues: if you are looking for something typically Florentine, search among the (pricey) shops on the Ponte Vecchio.

Ponte Vecchio
Jewellery and gold works fill the small shops that overhang the Ponte Vecchio and it is a fitting tribute that a bronze bust of Benvenuti Cellini, the city's most famous master goldsmith, stands in the centre. Through war and flooding, the Ponte Vecchio has become the enduring symbol of a city which survives and thrives.

The Centuries
In English we talk of the 1300s, the 1400s, the 1500s or the 1600s. In Italian these centuries are known as *trecento*, *quattrocento*, *cinquecento* and *seicento*. The Renaissance began in the early *quattrocento*, reached its height in the late *quattrocento* and early *cinquecento*, while Medieval art is *trecento* and, on rarer occasions, *duecento*, from the 1200s. This system continues up to the *novecento*, the 1900s, falling short of our present era, which is *contemporaneo*.

See Map C–E1 ★★★

Palazzo Medici-Riccardi
🕘 09:00–19:00 daily but closed Wed
✉ Palazzo Medici-Riccardi, via Cavour 3
☎ 055 2760340
🖱 info@palazzo-medici.it
🖥 www.palazzo-medici.it
🚌 see page 49
🍴 restaurants and cafés in Via Cavour, or nearby in Piazza del Duomo.

Opposite: The Crucifixion, *as depicted by the famous painter, Fra Angelico, hangs in the San Marco's Chapterhouse.*
Below: *Gracious Palazzo Medici-Riccardi – within its walls is the Cappella dei Magi, a jewel of a Renaissance chapel.*

PALAZZO MEDICI-RICCARDI

As the Prefecture occupies this imposingly austere palace (commissioned by Medici forefather, Cosimo the Elder and executed by Michelozzo, though sold to the Riccardi) entrance is virtually restricted to the **Cappella dei Magi**. This tiny religious building is, however, a gem of Renaissance decoration and was started in 1459 by painter Benozzo Gozzoli.

Powerful and breathtaking (perhaps more so because of its diminuitive size) the *Chapel of the Magi* is entirely painted with frescoes, a colourful mosaic of biblical scenes in which Florentine society appear in the guise of illustrative personages. Lorenzo appears as one of the Magi in the fresco **Processione dei Magi**, while his father Piero the Gouty is portrayed behind him on a white horse. Even Gozzoli found a space to include his own portrait; he wears a cap inscribed with the words *opus Benotii*, leaving no doubt as to his authorship. Thanks to

the meticulous detail and the incidental decoration seen in the figures, much about 15th century customs and costumes in Italy can be confirmed. The artist's treatment of the distant hills and forests is delightfully inaccurate but provides a foil for the far more important foreground figures.

See Map B–G4   ★★★

CONVENTO DI SAN MARCO

This Dominican convent, attached to the Church of San Marco, was built in 1436 for Cosimo I by **Michelozzo**, Cosimo's favourite architect (it was he who also designed the library). Its simple plan is a foil for the famous frescoes executed by one of its more celebrated painter-brothers, **Fra Angelico**, who arrived from St Domenico in Fiesole.

Fra Angelico went on to become a very successful painter and was canonized in 1983. **Antonius** was the prior here in the 1450s, while **Girolamo Savonarola** (*see* panel, this page) took the office in the late 1490s. Thereafter their paths diverged. Antonius eventually went on to beatification, while Savonarola burned at the stake. Monuments to both are in the church.

Fra Angelico's works are to be found in the Pilgrims' Hospice, where he painted the *Last Judgement* and also the charming *Linaoli Madonna* for the Guild of Linen Merchants. In the Chapterhouse he executed *The Crucifixion* (there is also a *Last Supper* by **Ghirlandaio** painted for the refectory, now the bookshop).

On the first floor is the familiar fresco of Fra Angelico's **Annunciation**. Beyond, the monks had their 44 individual cells, all decorated by Fra Angelico and his assistants. The austere quarters used by Savonarola contain a few simple possessions used by the prior.

Above: *The in-imitable statue of* David, *by Michelangelo.*

See Map C–F1 ★★★

GALLERIA DELL'ACCADEMIA

It is Michelangelo's famous statue of *David* which brings most visitors to this gallery but it also houses other important works by this genius and an art gallery of Florentine painting from the 1200s–1800s.

Among **Michelangelo**'s works are the four out of the six slaves intended for the tomb of **Julius II** in Rome and an unfinished *St Matthew*, destined for the Duomo. This collection of the artist's largely unfinished works show how he visualized the three dimensional pieces, and how he began the hard task of chiselling away marble to create the free-standing pieces. The sculptor's *David* stands in a specially built atrium, a young man about to slay a giant, and an allegory for the powerful Florentine city-state in *cinquecento* Italy. A tribute to its flawless beauty and fine Carrara marble, this statue is copied in all conceivable sizes and yet none ever capture the beauty of the original. It was intended for Piazza della Signoria and a replica of this sculpture – somewhat the worse for droppings of the pigeons that rest on his head – stands there. Sometimes with the crowds in the gallery, it is easier to study this work in the piazza itself.

The gallery also houses a good collection of musical instruments, some interesting examples of Florentine decorative arts, and a gallery of 15th and 16th century Italian paintings located in the four-room Pinacoteca.

Galleria dell'Accademia
🕐 08:15–18:50 Tue–Sun in winter; 08:15–18:50 Tue–Fri and Sun, 08:15–22:00 Sat during summer.
✉ via Ricasoli 60
☎ 055 1388609
🖥 www.sbas.firenze.it/accademia/
💰 entry fee

PIAZZA DELLA SANTISSIMA ANNUNZIATA

See Map C–G1 ★ ★ ★

PIAZZA DELLA SANTISSIMA ANNUNZIATA

This attractive porticoed piazza was designed by Brunelleschi and its centre is marked by a fine Giambologna equestrian statue of Grand Duke **Fernando I**. There are a number of interesting buildings to look at around the piazza.

Another conversion by **Michelozzo**, the church of **Santissima Annunziata** has some well-restored frescoes in its **Chiostrino dei Voti**, dating from the *cinquecento* but executed by some of the biggest names then around – **Andrea del Sarto**, **Pontormo**, and **Rosso Fiorentino** among others.

On the southeastern side of the piazza, Brunelleschi designed the **Ospedale degli Innocenti**, a charitable hospital for foundlings and, surprisingly, it still functions as an orphanage. Raised by a flight of steps above the square, the 10 slender grey columns running along its length support a nine-arch colonnade – a beautiful piece of architecture, which the throngs of sprawling students seated below rarely appreciate. Blue and white ceramic roundels depicting infants, the work of **Andrea della Robbia**, decorate the space between the arches. Inside, an art gallery contains 14–17th century work by Florentine painters and local sculptors.

Santissima Annunziata
🕐 07:30–12:30 and 16:00–18:30 daily
☎ 055 2398034
✉ Piazza della Santissima Annunziata
💻 www.arca.net.db/musei/innocent.htm
💰 free

Ospedale degli Innocenti
🕐 08:30–14:00 Thu–Tue
☎ 055 2491708
✉ Piazza della Santissima Annunziata
💻 Same as above
💰 free

Below: *Ospedale degli Innocenti was designed by Brunelleschi.*

Above: *The dark grey stone chosen by Michelangelo gives a note of grandeur to the unusual stairs at the Laurenziana Library.*

The Medici Dynasty
From humble merchants to Grand Dukes to Queens, the Medici influenced history and the fortunes of more than just Florence.
Cosimo il Vecchio (Cosimo the Elder), 1389–1464
Piero il Gottoso (Piero the Gouty), 1414–1469
Lorenzo il Magnifico (Lorenzo the Magnificent), 1449–1492
Giovanni de Medici (Pope Leo X), 1475–1521
Lorenzo II (Duke of Urbino), 1492–1519
Francesco I, Grand Duke, 1541–1587
Catherine de Medici (married King Henri II), Queen of France, 1519–1589
Maria de Medici (widow of Henri IV), 1573-1642.

☼ See Map C–D2	★★★

SAN LORENZO

The area around the church of San Lorenzo held particular importance to the Medici family: it was their parish, their local church, and Cosimo commissioned his family residence there in 1444.

The church we see today (behind the grey exterior still awaiting its marble finish) stands on the site of a previous paleo-Christian chapel. It is one of the most important churches in the city and its re-strained elegance is the hallmark of earlier Medici commissions. In 1420 Brunelleschi remodelled the church with a nave and two aisles and included groundbreaking curved arches, Corinthian columns, pilasters, un-adorned surfaces and decorative cornices. Head for the **Sagrestia Vecchia**, the Old Sacristy, designed by Brunelleschi and decorated by **Donatello**, admiring the mar-vellous bronze doors as you enter, and enjoying the calm atmosphere created by the use of grey *pietra serena* stone and light coloured walls. **Taddeo Gaddi** painted the triptych *Madonna and Child*. Back in the church itself there is an attractive *Annunciation* by **Filippo Lippi**. Donatello is buried nearby.

The **Biblioteca Medicea Laurenziana** is another masterpiece. It contains some 10,000 priceless, original works by the Ancients (including **Virgil**), as well as texts by Petrarch and Machiavelli, and Lorenzo the Magnificent's own *Book of Hours*. The sombre but infinitely graceful vestibule was the work of **Michelangelo**, executed by Ammannati.

See Map C–D2 | ★★

CAPPELLE MEDICEE

The Medici Chapel was **Michelangelo**'s first architectural commission. You enter via the later **Cappella dei Principi**, the dark marble mausoleum to the Grand Dukes and continue on the **Sagrestia Nuova**. He began work on this New Sacristy in 1521, after having worked on the façade of the church. For five long years Michelangelo laboured in the quarries over the architectural details for this room but the Medicis cancelled his contract for the façade, replacing it with their more pressing need for a suitable family chapel and mausoleum.

This chapel intended as the last resting place for Medici family members includes the tombs of **Lorenzo the Magnificent**, and his brother **Giuliano**. It is grandiose, solemn and yet surprisingly beautiful – thanks to Michelangelo's superb and imaginative allegorical figures who lounge across the monumental tombs. Don't miss this artist's recently-discovered charcoal drawings, displayed in a nearby room.

Cappelle Medicee
🕐 08:15–17:00
Tue–Sat, 08:15–17:00
1st, 3rd and 5th Sun
each month, 08:15–
13:50 holidays
✉ Piazza Madonna
degli Aldobrandini
🖥 www.sbas.firenze.it.
cappellemedicee
🔔 entry fee
🍴 plenty of restaurants and cafés nearby

Biblioteca Medicea Laurenziana
🕐 10:00–17:00
Mon–Sat
✉ Piazza San Lorenzo
☎ 055 216634
🖥 www.arca.net/db/
chiese/lorenzo.htm
🔔 Entry fee
🍴 restaurants in the square and nearby

Below: *Michelangelo's* Night and Day *languish on one of the Medici tombs.*

Below: *Santa Maria Novella offers a rich repository of art.*

⚙ *See Map C–B2* | ★★

SANTA MARIA NOVELLA

The gloriously ornate green and white marble façade of this Dominican church dominates the square of the same name. Humanist architect **Alberti** complemented **Jacopo Talenti**'s Gothic lower half of the façade with a fine Renaissance upper section. It is one of Florence's most important buildings. Take time to study it from the obelisks (resting on sculptor **Giambologna**'s bronze tortoises!) in the gardens of the square before entering this rich church. The existing religious complex, complete with cloisters, was constructed in the 14th and 15th century and was funded by the wealthy **Rucellai** family. Inside, there are finely decorated chapels built by a number of prominent Florentine families: the **Bardi**, **Strozzi** and **Rucellai**. Among the artistic treasures, **Masaccio** painted a fine *Trinità* which was to influence the next generation of great painters; Domenico **Ghirlandaio** painted a magnificent and extensive fresco cycle of the *Life of the Virgin* and *Life of St John the Baptist*, probably his finest work; **Paolo Uccello** painted some excellent frescoes in the Chiostro Verde, and in the **Cappellone degli Spagnoli** there are mid-*quattrocento* frescoes by **Andrea Firenza**.

<u>**Santa Maria Novella**</u>
🕑 09:30–17:00 Mon–Thu and Sat, 13:00–17:00 Fri and Sun or holidays
✉ Piazza di Santa Maria Novella
☎ 055 215918
🖥 www.arca.net.db/musei/novella.htm
👟 Entry fee
🍽 There are many restaurants and cafés in the piazza, near the station or towards the Duomo.

☆ See Map B–E5 | ★★

CAPPELLA BRANCACCI

Albsolutely not to be missed is this chapel in Santa Maria del Carmine just a few minutes' walk west of Piazza Santo Spirito. Commissioned by the Brancacci, local silk merchants, the frescoes which adorn the chapel show the hand of three painters: **Masolino** who began the work, the later artist **Filippino Lippi**, and those executed in 1427 depicting the life of Saint Peter, by the young master, **Masaccio** (1421–28, *see* page 15 for details of his short but influential life). The chapel is reached through the cloisters.

Masaccio's innovative frescoes had a profound effect on future generations – **Vasari** documented this in his *Lives of the Great Artists*. Thanks to his friendship with architect Brunelleschi and sculptor Donatello, Masaccio grasped many concepts of plasticity, architecture and realism. Just look at the expression of grief as *Adam and Eve* are expelled from Paradise; the plasticity of those elegant city figures and their fine costumes and the feeling of three dimensional space between buildings. All this was achieved at a time when Masaccio's contemporaries were capable of little more than stiff profiles and 'toy town' renditions of buildings. These frescoes confirm Masaccio's position as one of the founders of modern painting.

Cappella Brancacci
🕐 10:00–17:00 Mon, Wed–Sat, 13:00–17:00 Sun
✉ Piazza del Carmine
☎ 055 2382195
🖥 www.arca.net.db/musei/brancacc.htm
💰 Entry fee
🍽 There are cafés in the square and restaurants in Piazza Santo Spirito, some five minutes walk from here.

Below: *The small Brancacci chapel chronicles a turning point in art history between the beautiful yet staid work of Masolino and the dynamic painting of his pupil, Masaccio.*

See Map C–G5

★★

PIAZZA DI SANTA CROCE

This large and slightly run-down piazza is a real neighbourhood area of residential Florence and has, as its focal point, the Franciscan basilica of the same name.

The church of **Santa Croce** was possibly conceived by Arnolfo di Cambio in 1294 and completed 150 years later by Vasari who remodelled parts of it in 1560. It was a popular basilica with many of the wealthy Florentine banking families (as witnessed by their various chapels) and some notable personalities. **Alberti**, **Giotto**, **Galileo Galilei**, **Lorenzo Ghiberti** and **Michelangelo** are all buried here. There are, in addition, memorials to **Dante**, **Machiavelli** and playwright **Vittorio Alfieri**. But it is the frescoes in the family **chapels**, sculptural works and the architecture of the **Pazzi Chapel** which bring most visitors here.

Around 1320 **Giotto** was commissioned to paint frescoes in four chapels but the only surviving works are *Life of St Francis* for the **Bardi Chapel**, *Life of St John the Baptist and St John the Evangelist* in the **Peruzzi Chapel** and the *Coronation of the Virgin* in the **Baroncelli Chapel** (now believed to be by Giotto's workshop). This was an enormous undertaking for the artist and it is evident that he had help from his followers in completing the task. Take a moment to look at

Piazza di Santa Croce
🍽 There are plenty of cafés and restaurants in the piazza and nearby.

Church of Santa Croce
🕐 09:30–12:30 and 15:00–17:30 Mon–Sat, 15:00–17:30 Sun in winter; additionally 09:30–17:30 in summer
✉ Piazza di Santa Croce
🖥 www.arca.net.db/ chiese/scroce.htm
💰 Free entry

Cappella de' Pazzi (chapel and museum)
🕐 10:00–17:00 Thu–Tue in winter, 10:00–18:00 Thu–Tue during the summer
✉ Piazza di Santa Croce
☎ 055 244619
🖥 www.arca.net.db/ musei/pazzichp.htm
💰 Free entrance for under 12s

Below: *The façade of Santa Croce dominates the large, open piazza of the same name.*

Donatello's *Crucifixion* in the second Bardi Chapel (in the northern transept). It apparently caused great upsets in artistic circles when first displayed, as it was too realistic.

Above: *The serene exterior of the Pazzi Chapel.*

Work from the church is housed in the excellent **Museo dell'Opera di Santa Croce**, close to the Cloisters. Here **Cimabue's** carefully restored **Crucifix**, badly damaged in the 1966 flood, now hangs proudly in the refectory. Frescoes by **Taddeo Gaddi** (d1366) and his contemporary, **Orcagna,** which were removed from the church when Vasari remodelled the nave, are also on display. Another very impressive work is **Donatello's** *St Louis of Toulouse*, intended for Orsanmichele.

At the far end of the Cloisters (a late work by Brunelleschi) stands the **Cappella de' Pazzi**, or Pazzi Chapel. It was commissioned by the wealthy Pazzi family and designed by **Brunelleschi** who worked on it until 1445. It is probably one of his most successful works for, in its simplicity, it has immense harmony. The colour scheme is reduced to grey (travertine) and cream (stucco), the floor plan is a square covered by a dome, with a rectangular apse. **Luca della Robbia** was responsible for the wonderful polychrome terracotta decoration. The **Large Cloisters** were also a late and fine Brunelleschi work.

> ### *Calcio Storico*
> Dressed in bulbous Renaissance costumes, two teams take to Piazza di Santa Croce which, for the event, has become a sand-filled arena. Each team representing a district comprises 27 players and the object is to get the ball into the opponents goal. It's a mixture of football, rugby and push-and-shove where feet, heads and fists are all means to the end. Caparisoned horses, noble riders and colourful supporters egg on their teams or deride their adversaries. The game dates back to 1530.

HIGHLIGHTS

Below: *A ceiling by Pietro da Cortona in the Pitti Palace.*

 See Map C–B6 ★

PIAZZA DE' PITTI

This large square, uniting Via Guicciardini and Via Romana, is dominated by the palace of the same name.

One of the largest palaces in Florence, though not necessarily one of the most beautiful, the **Palazzo Pitti** now houses various interesting museums. The palace was started in 1458 for Luca Pitti, a wealthy merchant and banker, though it later passed into Medici hands and was converted by Ammannati, providing the family and its heirs with a residence for more than 300 years. Over the centuries, the gardens and two wings were added.

Five museums occupy the palace. Most spectacular is the **Galleria Palatina**. Amid the generously and heavily-decorated rooms are some remarkable paintings and original ceilings, including those by **Pietro da Cortona** decorating the reception rooms and the museum's enviable collection of works by **Raphael** and **Titian**.

Look out for the intricate *pietra dura* tables made from exquisitely crafted coloured stone, and the stunning crystal chandeliers. Of the paintings, head for the magnificent **Portrait of a Gentleman** (by Pietro Aretino) and *The Concert* by **Titian**; *La Velata* (the Veiled Lady) and the **Madonnas** – the round *Madonna della Seggiola*, *Madonna dell'Impannata* and

Galleria Palatina
🕐 08:15–18:50 Tue–Sun, and additionally 08:15– 22:00 Sat in summer
✉ Piazza de' Pitti
☎ 055 2388614
🖥 www.arca.net.db/musei/palatine.htm

Galleria d'Arte Moderna
🕐 08:15–13:50 Tue–Sun, plus 2nd and 4th Mon each month (closed 2nd and 4th Sun each month)
✉ Piazza de' Pitti
☎ 055 2388616
🖥 www.sbas.firenze.it/gam

Galleria del Costume
🕐 08:15–13:50 Tue–Sun, plus 2nd and 4th Mon each month (closed 2nd and 4th Sun each month)
✉ Piazza de' Pitti
☎ 055 2388713

Museo degli Argenti
🕐 08:15–13:50
Tue–Sun, plus 2nd and
4th Mon each month
(closed 2nd and 4th
Sun each month)
✉ Piazza de' Pitti
☎ 055 2388709/761

**Museo delle
Porcellane**
🕐 08:15–13:50
Tue–Sun, plus 2nd and
4th Mon each month
(closed 2nd and 4th
Sun each month)
✉ Giardino di Boboli
☎ 055 2388709
🖥 www.sbas.
firenze.it/mdp
ℹ There is an entry
fee for all museums.
🍽 There are several
restaurants and cafés
nearby.

Madonna della Granduca – all four by **Raphael**; the sublime *Venus* by **Canova**; the uncomfortably realistic *Giuditta* holding Holofernes's head by **Allori**; portrait works by **Rubens**, **Velázquez**, **Tintoretto** and **Van Dyck**; and a late, brooding **Caravaggio**.

The **Galleria d'Arte Moderna**, in another wing, has Tuscan works from the 18th to 20th century. Take a look at the paintings from the **Machciaioli Movement**, a school of thought contemporary with the French Impressionists, and for whom nature, realism and the impression of a scene were rendered by *macchia* – marks or daubs of paint. The best exponents of this movement were **Nino Costa** (1826–1903), **Giovanni Fattori** (1825–1908), **Silvestro Lega** (1826–95) and **Telemaco Signorini** (1835–1901).

The **Apartamenti Reali**, or State Rooms, which share the same *piano nobile* floor, are also open to the public. They were occupied by the Medici and Lorraine Grand Dukes and then, in the late 1800s, by the Savoy family. They have been restored to reflect this époque and show fine furniture.

The **Galleria del Costume** (outlining the history of costume) and the **Museo degli Argenti** are of interest. The latter holds a large collection of silverware, decorative items and *pietra dura* vases inlaid with stone. Porcelain lovers shouldn't miss the well-displayed **Museo delle Porcellane** in the Boboli Garden.

Below: *Five excellent museums are housed in the Pitti Palace complex.*

Above: *Domenico Ghirlandaio was noted for painting several fine renditions of* The Last Supper – *this is the one in the refectory of Ognissanti church.*

Brunelleschi
Born 1377, Filippo Brunelleschi trained as a goldsmith and sculptor in Florence. His contributions to the world of art lay in his understanding and use of perspective to create the illusion of distance, in both architecture and in painting. Among his best known works are the **Foundlings Hospital** (an early architectural commission dating from 1421), **Duomo**, **Santo Spirito**, **San Lorenzo** and the **Cappella de' Pazzi**. In 1433 he spent a long time in Rome, and came back to Florence with renewed ideas about the use of classical architecture. He died 1466.

Churches
Ognissanti

All Saints' church, or Ognissanti, is located about halfway down Borgo Ognissanti. The original 13th-century church was rebuilt during the 17th century. Botticelli is buried here, but it is the important frescoes in the church which attract most visitors. Highlight of the building is the *The Last Supper* by **Domenico Ghirlandaio** (1449–94), a beautiful painting in the church's refectory. Though not a highly innovative artist, Ghirlandaio was a popular one and in this masterfully lit rendition he uses perspective and very naturalistic poses to create the illusion of the Supper in an alcove. He also painted the *St Jerome*.
✉ *Borgo Ognissanti*, ☎ *055 2396802.*

Chiesa di Santo Spirito

This run-down church is located in the large square of the same name, a popular venue for neighbourhood socializing. The church was designed by **Brunelleschi** (*see* panel, this page), though he died long before it was completed. Inside, there are a number of interesting works of art including a fine painting by Filippino Lippi (1457–1504), and the impressive late 15th-century sacristy by Giuliano da Sangallo.
✉ *Piazza Santo Spirito*, ☎ *055 287043.*

Orsanmichele

If the architecture of this church appears to be a little unusual, it is because it was originally conceived as a loggia and granary and was designed by **Neri di Fioravanti** and **Francesco Talenti** in the 14th century; part of it was used as a chapel in the 15th century. It has a pleasant, squarish interior with a fine sculpted, Gothic altarpiece by **Andrea Orcagna** but its major interest lies in the wonderful display of individual statuary which once decorated the external niches (many are copies of originals which have been moved, for protection, either inside or to museums) depicting the patron saints of various Florentine guilds and executed by some of the Renaissance's biggest names. Here were **bronze statues** by Lorenzo Ghiberti and Donatello, as well as works by Nanni di Banco, Luca della Robbia, Bernardo Daddi, Simone Talenti, Verrocchio and Giovanni Tedesco.

✉ *Via Arte della Lana*,
☎ *055 284944*,
🕓 *09:00–12:00 and 16:00–18:00 Mon–Fri, 09:00–13:00 and 16:00–18:00 Sat–Sun.*

San Miniato al Monte

Below the Piazzale Michelangelo and accessible up a monumental staircase is the delightful church of San Miniato. The views are very good from here. This small building was erected on the site of an earlier chapel but it was in the 11th century that a Benedictine monastery was built on the hillside. Dedicated to the martyr Minias, who was beheaded by the Romans and possibly buried here, it served as the order's church. The harmonious façade, decorated in geometric green and white marble and topped by a mosaic, hides a Romanesque

Below: *Orsanmichele is noted for its fine external sculpture.*

Opposite: *Perseus holds high the head of Medusa – Cellini's sculpture stands in the Loggia della Signoria.*
Below: *Crowds pack the Loggia del Mercato Nuovo, a popular souvenir market at the corner of Via Por Santa Maria and Via Porta Rossa.*

church laid out in a basilica form. Among its treasures are the (much renovated) painted wooden ceiling, the fancy marble floor, and the Chapel of the Cardinal of Portugal, encompassing the Cardinal's tomb by Antonio Rossellino and decorated by glazed terracotta, the work of Luca della Robbia.
✉ *Via Monte alle Croci,* ☎ *055 2342731,* 🕐 *08:00–12:30 and 14:30–19:30 daily in winter, 08:30–19:30 daily in summer.*

Badia Fiorentina

Just opposite the Museo del Bargello is the Badia Fiorentina, the Benedictine church of an abbey founded in 978 – though its **medieval tower** was added after 1310 – while the church was extensively remodelled in the 17th century. The church's most interesting features are its coffered wooden ceiling and Filippo Lippi's *Madonna Appearing to St Bernard*. The church is rarely open, except for the scheduled religious services.
✉ *via del Proconsulo,* 🕐 *not open to public.*

Loggias and Palaces

Loggia del Mercato Nuovo

This 16th-century loggia was built to house the produce market. It now shelters a popular market (also called the **Mercato del Porcellino**, after the bronze fountain with the form of a large

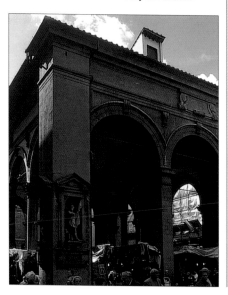

boar) selling straw goods, leather, and souvenirs.

✉ via Porta Rossa, ⊕ daily, all hours.

Loggia dei Lanzi

Also known as the Loggia della Signoria (see page 18), this loggia shelters some exquisite sculpture and is a popular place to sit.

✉ Piazza della Signoria, ⊕ daily, all hours.

Palazzo and Museo Davanzati

This medieval palace was bought by Bernardo Davanzati in the 16th century and, in keeping with the times, he added the fashionable loggia level at the top. In contrast to this, the odd-looking Orsanmichele (see page 34) started life as a loggia but its walls were later filled in giving it its present form.

✉ via Porta Rossa 13, ☎ 055 2388610, ⊕ 08:15–13:45 on the

1st, 3rd and 5th Sun of each month as well as the 2nd and 4th Mon of the month.

Museums and Galleries
Museo Bardini

The eclectic collection in this museum used to belong to Stefano Bardini, who constructed the palace to house his various art acquisitions, and bequeathed it to the city on his death in 1923. The furnishings, paintings, arms, decorative items and sculpture belong to a wealth of different eras but among the treasures are a **Donatello** terracotta of a Madonna and Child and a statue by **Tino da Camaino** of Charity.

✉ piazza de' Mozzi 1, ☎ 055 2342427, ⊕ 09:00–13:00 Thu–Tue.

Museo Horne

The Horne Museum is housed in the Palazzo Corsi. It has an interesting collection of

Famous Artists
Cimabue, ca. 1240–1302, painter
Donatello, ca. 1385–1466, sculptor
Filippo Brunelleschi, 1377–1446, Florentine sculptor, goldsmith and architect
Lorenzo Ghiberti, 1378–1455, Florentine sculptor
Giotto, 1266–1337, Florentine painter
Michelangelo (Buonarroti), 1475–1564, Florentine architect, sculptor and painter
Michelozzo, 1396–1472, sculptor and architect
Perugino, ca. 1445–1523, painter
Piero della Francesca, ca. 1410–92, painter
Bernardino Pinturicchio, 1454–1513, painter
Nicola Pisano, 1225–78, and **Giovanni Pisano**, ca. 1245–1314, father and son sculptors
Raphael (Sanzio), 1483–1520, painter
Luca della Robbia, 1399–1482, sculptor

Art Terms

Abbazia – abbey
Badia – abbey
Basilica – church or cathedral with nave, no separate aisles
Cappella – chapel
Cenacolo – both a refectory and a painting of the *Last Supper*
Chiesa – church
Cupola – dome
Duomo – cathedral
Eremito – hermitage
Fresco – a wall painting, done in wet plaster
Intarsia – inlaid work in stone, wood or metal
Opera – artistic works
Pieve – parish church
Putto – small cherub, often nearly nude
Tondo – a sculpture in low relief or a round painting

Museums

Because of the crowds and long queues, the state museums now offer a prebooking service for tickets; ☎ 055 294883, to reserve and pay with a credit card in the following popular museums:
Galleria d'Arte Moderna
Galleria degli Uffizi
Cappelle Medicee
Galleria dell'Accademia
Museo Archeologico
Museo del Bargello
Museo di San Marco

ceramics, furniture, sculpture and some paintings donated by art historian and collector, Englishman Herbert Horne. Look out for **Giotto**'s *St Stephen*, **Beccafumi**'s *tondo* of the *Holy Family*, **Piero di Cosimo**'s *tondo* of the *Madonna with Christ*, and some of the fine furniture (a 15th-century inlaid intarsia bench from a sacristy), as well as Renaissance domestic utensils and maiolica.
✉ *via de' Benci 6*,
☎ *055 244661*,
⏰ *09:00–13:00 Mon–Sat.*

Museo Archeologico

This museum offers a respite from the myriad works of the Medieval and Renaissance eras. Here you'll step back into Etruscan and Roman times and see such **bronze masterpieces** as the *Chimera* (4th century BC) and the Etruscan vase, known as the François Vase. There are also fine exhibits of ceramics, Egyptian sarcophagi and Roman sculpture.
✉ *via della Colonna 38*, ☎ *055 244661*,
✆ *sat@commune. firenze.it*
💻 *www.commune. firenze.it/soggetti/sat/ didattica/museo/html*
⏰ *14:00–19:00 Mon, 08:30–19:00 Tue and Thu, 08:30–14:00 Wed, Fri–Sun.*

Opificio delle Pietre Dure

It's an interesting detour to visit this museum dedicated to the ancient art of *pietra dura* (hard stone), achieved by slicing **semi-precious** and **coloured stones** into small pieces to create designs on furniture and other decorative arts. This classical art had fallen out of favour until Lorenzo the Magnificent began to commission several such works, and subsequently the workshops began to thrive. This museum shows how the semi-precious stones are cut, exhibits various unfinished panels and provides an interesting reconstruction of a typical *pietra dura* workshop.

✉ *via degli Alfani 78,*
☎ *055 265111,*
📧 *imss@imss.fi.it*
🖥 *www.imss.firenze.it.ipietrdu.htm*
🕐 *08:15–14:00 Mon–Wed and Fri–Sat, 08:15–19:00 Thu.*

Museo Stibbert

This museum is the legacy of Frederick Stibbert (1838–1906), an avid collector. He designed the rooms in this building to house his collection, in particular the magnificent exhibits of **armour**, **weapons** and **costume**. The gardens of the museum, likewise the creation of Stibbert, are open to the public.

✉ *via Stibbert 26,*
☎ *055 219432,*
🕐 *10:00–14:00 Mon–Wed, 10:00–18:00 Fri–Sun*

Museo dell'Opera del Duomo

Many sculptural items from the Cathedral, Baptistery and Campanile have been moved to this museum which, appropriately, occupies the same building as the Cathedral Workshop has done since Brunelleschi's day. Housing the Duomo's treasures, this museum offers a fine collection of sculpture. Look out for works by **Jacopo della Quercia** and **Giovanni Pisano**, and study **Donatello's**

Below: *Visitors to the Museo dell'Opera del Duomo discuss the various renditions of St John the Baptist.*

tondo of *Mother and Child*. Don't miss pride of place: the *Maestà* by **Duccio**. Originally from the high altar, this painting was backed by 26 smaller panels depicting scenes from the life of Christ. It was an innovative work, glistening with gold and vibrating with colours which caused a stir when it was carried from studio to Duomo. Highlights of this museum are Michelangelo's *Pietà*, finished by a pupil of his, as well as works by Andrea Pisano and Giotto.

✉ piazza del Duomo 9, ☎ 055 2302885, 🕒 09:00–19:30 Mon–Sat, 09:00–13:40 Sun.

Museo Marino Marini

This museum, located in the deconsecrated church of San Pancrazio, has a fine exhibition of sculpture by this talented painter turned sculptor. Born in 1901, he trained in Florence but worked mainly in Milan. The artist's interest in Etruscan and Classical Greek art during the 1930s influenced some of his most familiar work, especially those of man and horse, which he executed in both wood and bronze. One of these raises its claws when the gate is opened.
✉ Piazza San Pancrazio,
☎ 055 219432,
✉ info@
museomarinomarini.it
🖥 www.
museomarinomarini.it
🕒 10:00–17:00
Mon–Sat.

Sinagoga e Museo Ebraico

Known as the major temple, Florence's sinagogue was based on the Byzantine design – a domed, Greek cross – that formed Santa Sophia, in former Constantinople. Enter via the Silent Garden in front of the building. The interior is richly decorated with mosaics (unlike Santa Sophia). There are some items of furniture which have survived from the Old Ghetto, near Piazza della Repubblica, where Jews were forced to live between the late 16th and mid-19th centuries. The museum reconstructs the history of Judaism in Florence, exhibits and interesting wooden maquette of the Ghetto area, and has a good collection of ceremonial items.

✉ *via Farini 4,*
☎ *055 2346654,*
🕓 *10:00–13:00 and 14:00–16:00 Sun–Thu, 10:00–13:00 Fri.*

Museo di Storia della Scienza

Adjoining the Uffizi, the Museum of the History of Science is housed in the solid, Medieval **Palazzo Castellani**. Dedicated to the evolution of scientific knowledge and **instruments**, it exhibits many of the instruments made for the Medici *granduci* and some of **Galileo**'s possessions such as his telescope, compass and, more bizarrely, one of **his fingers** in a reliquary. The surgical instruments provide a parting reflection as to the unsophistication of medicine in the Medieval and Renaissance times.

✉ *piazza de' Guidici 1,*
☎ *055 265311,*

Above and opposite: *Displayed in the deconsecrated church of San Pacrazio, the large works of sculptor Marino Marini are shown in a spacious and congenial environment.*

DANTE ALIGHIERI

Dante Alighieri

Born 1265 in Florence to minor nobility and White Guelf sympathizers, Dante formed, with fellow poet, Guido Cavalacanti, a movement called the **Dolce Stil Nuovo**, Sweet New Style. As a young adult he fell in love with the even younger Beatrice Portinari, whom he eulogizes in many a written work. By 1300 he became the Florentine representative to the Pope. However, the Black Guelfs rose against the White Guelfs and Dante was thrown out of public office and condemned to death. His sentence was subsequently commuted to exile, and in 1302 he left Florence, never to return. It was during his exile that he wrote the masterpieces, **Divine Comedy** and **The Monarchy**. He died in Ravenna, aged 56.

🔆 *imss@imss.fi.it*
🖳 *www.imss.firenze.it*
🕒 *09:30–17:00 Mon and Wed–Fri, 09:30–13:00 Tue and Sat.*

Casa di Dante Alighieri

Just over the Via dei Proconsolo stands the dignified stone house where **Dante Alighieri** (*see* panel, left) was supposed to have been born in 1265. However, chased into exile for his political allegiance in 1302, he never lived here again. The Casa di Dante Alighieri is now a museum chronicling his life. Look at 'Dante's church', just opposite – a small yet tranquil retreat.
✉ *via Dante Alighieri and via Santa Margherita 1,*
☎ *055 219416,*
🕒 *10:00–18:00 Wed–Mon, 10:00–14:00 holidays.*

Casa Buonarroti

Michelangelo purchased three houses in 1508 and created one for himself.

On his death the property passed to his nephew. Today, the house has been re-organized to show off, on the first floor, works by the young Michelangelo and include a number of fascinating drawings.
✉ *via Ghibellina 70,*
☎ *055 241752,*
🕒 *09:30–14:00 Wed–Mon.*

Museo di 'Firenze Com'era'

'Florence as it was' is the odd name of this museum in the former convent of the Olbate nuns, behind the Duomo. The building once formed part of the Ospedale di Santa Maria Nuova, a hospital dating from 1286 and one which is still functioning. On display are paintings, engravings and maps. There are also some impressive lunettes showing the Medici villas.
✉ *via dell'Oriuolo 24,*
☎ *055 2616545,*
🕒 *09:00–14:00 Fri–Wed.*

Views
Forte di Belvedere
This large fort was commissioned by Ferdinando I and built by Buontalenti in 1590. It is only open to the public when exhibitions are staged but most people visit its grounds for the magnificent panoramic views of Florence and the Tuscan hills. It is also accessible from the Boboli Garden.
✉ *via del Forte di San Giorgio,* ⏰ *not open to public unless staging public exhibitions.*

Piazzale Michelangelo
This is the place to go (if you haven't climbed the Campanile or the Duomo) to put Florence into perspective. On a clear, pollution-free day, the city spreads out beneath you as a rust-coloured carpet of roofs, bisected by the Arno and enclosed by the foothills of the Apennines. It is a popular spot – vendors and tour groups crowd the large square – with a tribute to Michelangelo in its centre.
✉ *piazzale Michelangelo,* ⏰ *daily, all hours.*

Giardino di Boboli
One of Florence's favourite places to hang out, especially on Sundays, the Boboli Garden brings

Opposite: *A tribute to Florence's greatest scribe – Dante Alighieri.*
Below: *The superb view from Piazzale Michelangelo towards the Ponte Vecchio.*

The Idiot in Florence
Fyodor Mikhailovich Dostoevsky is remembered by a plaque at Piazza de' Pitti 22, just opposite the entrance to the Boboli Garden. The Russian writer sojourned in Florence in 1868–69, during which time he wrote *The Idiot*.

Below: *Giardino di Boboli, built by Cosimo I, is one of Florence's most popular parks.*

a breath of fresh air, cooling fountains and sculptural pleasure to the centre of town. The Gardens were commissioned in 1549 by **Cosimo I** who wanted to transform the hillside behind the Pitti Palace into a formal terraced garden. Plans were made by architect **Tribolo** who died before it was finished. It was subsequently continued by local favourites **Ammannati** and **Buontalenti**. The garden is divided into two main sections. The lower area is formally laid out on either side of a splendid avenue, the **Viottolone**, which rises in long gentle tiers between areas of evergreens, to the circular **Isolotto**. Over 150 statues line the walkways. The 17th-century amphitheatre was conceived and used as a venue for pageants. To enjoy the gardens to their fullest, walk through them and exit via the Forte di Belvedere for a spectacular view over Florence.

✉ *Palazzo Pitti, Piazza de' Pitti and Piazzale di Porta Romana, Via Porta Romana (Annalena Gate) or Forte di Belvedere,* ☎ *055 218741,* ☼ *daily, except on the first and last Monday of the month: 09:30–16:30 in winter, 09:00–19:30 in summer, 09:00–18:30 in spring and autumn.* ⌨ *www.firenze-oltrarno.net/english/arte/t-bob.html*

ACTIVITIES
Sport and Recreation

Activities other than art history or shopping are rather thin on the ground in Florence but of course there are alternatives. The most obvious spectator sport in this city is rowing: most days there are single skiffs on the River Arno, and the rowing club, just by the Ponte Vecchio, is popular with locals.

Florence has a good football team, **Fiorentina**. Games are played at their grounds, Stadio Comunale (see page 73).

Pedestrianized Florence is bike-friendly. There are even a number of bike routes to help ensure cyclists' safety. Currently a pilot scheme (*Mille e Una Bici*, or 1001 Bikes) is underway by the *Comune* of Florence, whereby for a nominal fee of around 1.6 Euros, would-be cyclists can hire a bike from one of the town's 16 main depot/parks. Alternatively, bikes can be hired from various organizations (see side panel). Bikes vary in size, sophistication and therefore price. Florence by Bike offer accompanied bike tours in town (and out into Tuscany) and also rent scooters.

Walking Tours
Palaces

Thanks to the pedestrianization of the city's central streets, Florence once again lends itself to walking, and this is by far the best way of seeing and appreciating the city. For an interesting tour that takes in some of Florence's most elegant palaces, start at **Piazza della Repubblica** (see

Florence by Bike
For bike and scooter rentals contact the following:

Florence by Bike
✉ via San Zanobia 120r/122r,
☎ 055 488992,
🖰 ecologica@dada.it
💻 www.florencebybike.it
🕐 09:00–19:30 daily

Manila Bike
✉ via Dossio 50,
☎ 055 715776.

Motorent
✉ via San Zanobi 9r,
☎ 055 490113.

Sim Pa
✉ piazza Mercato Centrale 42r,
☎ 055 210658.

Below: *Rowing is a popular pastime on the River Arno.*

Above: *The late 15th-century Palazzo Strozzi.*

Festivals
The **Calcio football game** held during June is a highlight. Teams dressed in 16th-century costumes battle it out in Piazza di Santa Croce. Fireworks launched from Piazzale Michelangelo mark the feast of **Saint John the Baptist** (24 June) while the **Scoppio del Carro** (the exploding of the cart), a Medieval religious festival surrounding an ox-drawn cart, is held on Easter Sunday outside the Duomo and culminates in a firework display. The participants are all dressed in colourful period costumes. On 7 September, the **Rificolona**, Lantern festival, is celebrated around town. The city's biennial **Antiques Fair** is held in odd-numbered years.

map C–D3), head west then turn left down Via de Sassetti, to find the **Palazzo Davanzati** on the right-hand corner with Via Porta Rossa. The narrow, high façade of this palace contains within its walls the **Museo dell'Antica Casa Fiorentina** (currently closed for restoration), a fine representation of 14th–16th-century Florentine interiors. Built originally in the 14th century for a rich merchant, Bernardo Davanzati bought it in the 16th century and added the fashionable loggia level at the top.

Next, follow Via Porto Rossa east and turn first right to reach Piazza Parte Guelfa. The 14th-century **Palazzo dei Capitani di Parte Guelfa** was the equivalent of Party Headquarters for the papal-supporting Guelfs. Note its outside staircase. Walk a block south then follow Borgo Santi Apostoli west to **Piazza Santa Trinità**. **Buontalenti** designed the 16th-century façade for the 14th-century church but notice how the 11th-century structure has been incorporated into the façade. Smart Via de' Tornabuoni, which runs from Santa Trinità to Via de' Panzani, has been in fashion ever since the Tornabuoni constructed their 14th-century palazzo here. Near neighbours include the **Spini-Feroni**, whose 13th-century mansion still survives at No.2, and the **Strozzis**, at the corner of Via degli Strozzi and Via de' Tornabuoni. **Palazzo Strozzi** has one of the most harmonious Renaissance façades and was built for Filippo Strozzi by a series of architects culminating in **Simone di Pollaiolo**.

At the north end of Via de' Tornabuoni, the Antinori family built their home,

Palazzo Antinori, giving the piazza the same name. This marvellous, relatively small palace was designed by Giuliano da Maiano in the mid-*quattrocento*.

Head south again (*see* Map C–B3) to the deconsecrated church, **San Pancrazio**, which now houses the **Museo Marino Marini** (*see* page 40). **Palazzo Rucellai**, on swish **Via della Vigna Nuova**, benefits from a lovely façade incorporating three architectural orders, and plenty of windows. It was built in the 1440s for Giovanni Rucellai by **Bernardo Rossellino**, from designs drawn up by Alberti. Today the new neighbours are also in the fashion business: Gucci, Armani and Valentino.

It's a couple of minutes walk from here to the huge 16th–17th-century **Palazzo Corsini**, a Baroque palace dominating the Lungarno Corsini (Map C–B4).

The Lungarno

Another popular walk is along the *lungarno*, the banks of the River Arno. Starting on the north bank of the **Ponte Vecchio**, and heading eastwards along the raised pavement beside the Lungarno delle Grazie, you'll walk above the rowing club and past the windows of the **Uffizi Gallery** (*see* page 14). Indeed, those windows up on the left afford a great view of the Ponte Vecchio while you are in the Uffizi itself. At the most easterly end of this large building is

> **Michelangelo**
> Lovers of Michelangelo's work could walk a route to take in his works starting at the artist's house, **Casa Buonarroti**, ✉ via Ghibellina 70, ☎ 055 241752, 🕐 mornings, closed Tue, to see his tomb in the church of **Santa Croce** (*see* page 30), to the **Cappelle Medicee** (*see* page 27) and **Biblioteca Medicea Laurenziana** (*see* page 26), the **Galleria dell'Accademia** (*see* page 24), the **Museo dell'Opera del Duomo** (*see* page 39), and perhaps the **Galleria degli Uffizi** (*see* page 14), and the **Galleria Palatina** (*see* page 32) in the Palazzo Pitti for the paintings.

Below: *Fashionable Via de' Tornabuoni.*

Florentine Bridges
Florence has seven city
bridges crossing its
stretch of the River
Arno. Five of these were
first erected some 700–
800 years ago but were
damaged or destroyed
during World War II.
The largely Medieval
Ponte Vecchio miracu-
lously – or by design –
escaped the bombing
which effectively flat-
tened the southern
suburbs of the city. Not
exactly a beauty, this
'Old Bridge' is perhaps
the city's most identifi-
able landmark.

Below: *Not only are
the wall-hung paint-
ings in the Palatine
Gallery of great
interest, but so too
are the ceilings,
furniture and the
architectural details.*

the **History of Science Museum** (*see* page
41). The Lungarno Generale Diaz continues
towards the modern **Ponte alle Grazie**, one
of the main bridges across the Arno. Here
the Arno appears faster flowing, the traffic
is less congested and, were you to rise early,
there'd be great sunrises to see over the
river. At the bridge, turn left into Via de'
Benci, where you will find **Museo Horne** on
your right (*see* page 37). If you cross the
Arno you'll come to Lungarno Torrigini and
Via de' Bardi. The more energetic visitor
might like to head on up to the **Forte di
Belvedere** or **Piazzale Michelangelo** (Map
B–F6/G6) for panoramic views of the city
(and return to the centre of Florence via
the **Boboli Garden** – *see* page 43).

The walk westwards along Lungarno is not
always along the river side, but you can dip
in and out of various restaurants and cafés to
get views. It rejoins the Ponte Vecchio at this
very busy intersection and becomes Borgo
San Jacopo. Two minutes' walk to the south
along Via Guicciardini, and you'll arrive at
Piazza de' Pitti, home to
the huge **Pitti Palace** with
its various museums (*see*
page 32). Back on the
Borgo, steal a minute
or two, by the Hotel
Lungarno, for good views
of the back of the famous
bridge before heading on
down to **Ponte Santa
Trinità**, where Borgo San
Jacopo is joined by Via
Maggio. It is just a two-
minute walk south from
there towards the church

of **Santo Spirito** (*see* page 34). From here walk west to the **Brancacci Chapel** (*see* page 29) in Piazza del Carmine. Retrace your steps and cross the river to Piazza Santa Trinità, an elegant square. **Palazzo Corsini** (*see* page 47) is just off to the left, while to the right Lungarno degli Acciaiuoli will return the pedestrian to the Ponte Vecchio.

The Last Supper

Another interesting themed walk follows the different examples of the *Cenacolo*, paintings and frescoes depicting the *Last Supper*. Many were painted in refectories, and Florence is particularly well-endowed with these scenes (*see* panel, this page).

Organized Tours

In 1565, Cosimo I invited his architect, **Giorgio Vasari**, to design a secret corridor to run from his residence, now known as the Palazzo Vecchio, via the Uffizi Gallery, past the church of Santa Felicità, across the Arno on the top level of the Ponte Vecchio, and into the Palazzo Pitti. This is known today as **Vasari's Corridor**. Lined with fine paintings, it allowed the prince to move unnoticed from palace to palace without mixing with *hoi polloi* and without fear of assassination. The Corridor is now open for guided tours. For further information, ☎ 055 2654321.

Professionally accompanied walks can also be arranged (minimum price is around 180 Euro for 1–2 people, 20 Euro for each subsequent person). For further information, contact **Sunny Tuscany**, ⌧ via della Colonna 21, ☎ 055 489231, 📠 055 2268522, ✆ sunnytuscany@fionline.it

---

The Cenacolo Trail
Ognissanti
⌧ borgo Ognissanti 42, ☎ 055 2396802, 🕘 Mon, Tue and Sat morning, 💰 entry free. Work by Ghirlandaio.

Santa Apollonia
⌧ via XXVII Aprile 1, ☎ 055 2388607, 🕘 mornings, closed Mon, 💰 entry free. Work by Andrea del Castagno.

San Marco
⌧ piazza San Marco 1, ☎ 055 23885, 🕘 mornings, closed Mon,. 💰 there is an entry fee. Work by Ghirlandaio.

Scalzo Cloisters
⌧ via Cavour 69, ☎ 055 2388604, 🕘 Mon and Thu morning, 💰 entry free. Work by Andrea del Sarto.

San Salvi
⌧ via San Salvi 16, ☎ 055 2388603, 🚌 Bus 6 from Duomo, 🕘 mornings, closed Mon, 💰 there is an entry fee. Work by Andrea del Sarto.

Santa Croce
⌧ piazza di Santa Croce 16, ☎ 055 244619, 🕘 morning and afternoon, closed Wed, 💰 there is an entry fee. Work by Taddeo Gaddi.

Santo Spirito
⌧ Piazza Santo Spirito, ☎ 055 287043, 🕘 mornings, closed Mon, 💰 there is an entry fee. Work by Andrea Orcagna.

Above: *A variety of leather goods can be found in the Mercato Nuovo.*

Shops

Armani
Classic, Italian fashion at its best.
✉ *via della Vigna Nuova 51r,*
☎ *055 219041,*
💻 *www.armani.com* ⏱ *15:30–19:30 Mon, 10:00–19:00 Tue–Sat.*

Bulgari
Jewellers to the well-heeled.
✉ *via de' Tornabuoni 61/63r,*
☎ *055 2396786,*
💻 *www.bulgari.com*
⏱ *15:00–19:30 Mon, 10:00–19:00 Tue–Sat.*

Emporio Armani
Affordable Armani fashion.
✉ *piazza Strozzi 16r,*
☎ *055 284315,*
💻 *www. emporioarmani.com*
⏱ *15:00–19.30 Mon, 10:00–19:00 Tue–Sat.*

Dolce & Gabbana
Smart and affordable Italian fashion and accessories.
✉ *via della Vigna Nuova 27,*
☎ *055 281003,*
⏱ *15:00–19:30 Mon, 10:00–19:00 Tue–Sat.*

Ferragamo
Florence's famous shoemakers, now known also for leather accessories.
✉ *via de' Tornabuoni 14r,* ☎ *055 292123,*
💻 *www. ferragamo.com*
⏱ *15:30–19:30 Mon, 09:30–19:30 Tue–Sat.*

Gianni Versace
Chic Italian fashion for the dedicated trendsetter.
✉ *via de' Tornabuoni 13–15r,* ☎ *055 282638,*
💻 *www. gianniversace.com*
⏱ *15:00–19:00 Mon, 10:00–19:00 Tue–Sat.*

Gucci

Classic fashion and must-have accessories.
✉ via de' Tornabuoni 73r, ☎ 055 264 011, 🖥 www.gucci.it
🕐 15:00–19:00 Mon, 10:00–19:00 Tue–Sat.

Prada

Spanish fashion know-how moves into Florence.
✉ via de' Tornabuoni 51/55r, 67r,
☎ 055 283439,
🖥 www.prada.com
🕐 15:00–19:00 Mon, 10:00–19:00 Tue–Sat.

Pucci

Florentine traditional *alta moda* for the well-dressed.
✉ via della Vigna Nuova 97r, ☎ 055 294028, 🕐 15:30–19:30 Mon, 10:00–13:00, 15:30–19:30 Tue–Sat.

Pusateri

Selection of gloves and prestige leather goods.
✉ via dei Calzaiuoli 25r, ☎ 055 214192.

Peruzzi

Leather goods (and tax-free advantages).
✉ borgo de' Greci 8–20r, or via dell' Anguillara 5–23r,
☎ 055 289039, ✆ 055 287619, ✉ info@peruzzispa.com 🖥 www.peruzzispa.com

Bi Bi

Affordable leather goods and accessories.
✉ via dell'Ariento 12r
☎ 055 2302400.

Mazzoni

For fine household linens and textiles.
✉ via Orsanmichele 14r, ☎ 055 215153.

Armando Poggi

Household ceramics, silverware and crystal.
✉ via dei Calzaiuoli 103r or via dei Calzaiuoli 116r,
☎ 055 211719, ✉ info@armandopoggi.it

Seeber

The German bookshop (with some English and Italian titles).
✉ via de' Tornabuoni 70r, ☎ 055 215697.

Feltrinelli

A premier publisher and good bookshop.
✉ via Cavour 12–20r,
☎ 055 2382652.

Alinari

Another of the country's best publishers; also a good bookshop.
✉ largo Alinari 15,
☎ 055 23951.

Il Viaggio

A bookshop specialising in guide and travel books.
✉ borgo degli Albizzi 21, ☎ 055 292085.

Erboristeria Inglese

Fabulous fragrances, soaps, gift items as well as traditional remedies.
✉ via de' Tornabuoni 19, ☎ 055 210628, ✉ info@erboristeria inglese.com

Profumeria Inglese

A marvellous old perfume store and beauty clinic with hundreds of fragrances.
✉ via de' Tornabuoni 97r, ☎ 055 289748.

Parione

Sells and ships decorative stationery, a Tuscan speciality.

✉ *via del Parione 10r,*
☎ *055 215684,*
🖥 *www.parione.it*

L'Antica Cantina del Chianti

Stock up here on local Chianti wines as well as wines from other regions of Italy.
✉ *piazza del Duomo 23r,* ☎ *055 282489.*

Enoteca Baldovino

A wine bar and wine shop with a good selection of Italy's better wines including most of the Tuscan greats.
✉ *via di San Guiseppe 18r,* ☎ *055 2347220.*

Millesimi

For a selection of Tuscan (and other European) wines.
✉ *borgo Tegloaio 33r,*
☎ *055 2654675,*
🖥 *www.millesimi.it*

Enoteca de' Giraldi

Stock up here on typical Tuscan produce, Italian ingredients and fine wines.
✉ *via de' Giraldi 4r,* ☎ *055 216518,*
🖥 *www.vinaio.com*

Coin

This department store is the place for household goods, though the fashion, etc, is inexpensive too.
✉ *via dei Calzaiuoli 56r,* ☎ *055 280531,*
🖥 *www.coin.it*
🕐 *09:30–20:00 Mon–Sat, 11:00–20:00 Sun.*

La Rinascente

A long-time favourite department store, sells a mix of fashion and householdware.
✉ *piazza della Repubblica 1,*
☎ *055 219113,*
🖥 *www.rinascente.it*
🕐 *09:00–21:00 Mon–Sat, 10:30–20:00 Sun.*

Principe

A scaled down version of their previous store, Principe on Via del Sole is not quite as impressive as it used to be, though still a decent store.
✉ *via del Sole 2 (Santa Maria Novella area),* ☎ *055 292765,*
🖥 *www. principedifirenze.it*
🕐 *15:30–19:30 Mon, 09:30–19:30 Tue–Sat.*

Markets

Mercato Centrale

Known as Mercato di San Lorenzo, this popular market is the most easily accessible one. The covered food section is the forte of Florentine housewives who set out early for the freshest produce. The clothes section opens slightly later and conducts a fierce business with particular attention to leather goods and clothing.
✉ *piazza del Mercato Centrale, and the streets around San Lorenzo,* 🕐 *08:30–19:00 Mon–Sat, while the food section is open 07:00–14:00 only.*

Mercato Nuovo

Also known as the Mercato del Porcellino, this is the place for souvenirs of Florence including alabaster, leather and straw items. The market overflows, nowadays, into the area around the Duomo.
✉ *under the historic Loggia Mercato Nuovo,* 🕐 *09:00–19:00 daily.*

Mercato di Sant'Ambrogio

This is the market for Florentines – the city's best buys in fresh produce and a good place for cheap clothes.

✉ *Piazza Ghiberti, near Santa Croce,* ⏰ *07:00–14:00 Mon–Sat.*

Mercato delle Pulci

Antique and bric-a-brac hunters should head for this market. It is a fun place to look through and a good place in which to find the occasional household bargain, perhaps an item of second-hand designer-wear or a would-be antique.

✉ *piazza dei Ciompi, behind Santa Croce,* ⏰ *09:00–19:00 Mon–Sat.*

Santo Spirito Flea Market

This is a good address for sifting through bric-a-brac.

✉ *piazza Santo Spirito,* ⏰ *08:00–18:00 on the 2nd and 3rd Sun each month.*

Mercato dei Pianti

Plant lovers should head for the Plant Market, which is always colourful, to pick up a bouquet or just enjoy the flowers.

✉ *piazza della Repubblica,* ⏰ *08:00–13:00 Thu.*

Mercato delle Cascine

For another Florentine experience, head out of the city centre to this market, a real mishmash of stalls catering specifically for a local clientele. Buses 1, 9, 12 or 13 travel to the Cascine.

✉ *parco delle Cascine, Viale Lincoln,* ⏰ *08:00–13:00 Tue.*

Above: *Worn down to gleaming bronze, the porcellino's snout attracts the caresses of practically all passersby, many of whom clamber for a photo beside this wild boar. Because of all the touching, the original has now been replaced by this excellent copy.*

Above: *Opulence and comfort are the standards of this landmark hotel overlooking the River Arno.*

WHERE TO STAY

In Florence there is accommodation to suit most purses but do be prepared for higher prices than in other European provincial towns – Italy has long since ceased being a budget destination.

Many of the city's hotels and pensions are privately owned – often in historic buildings – and are graded according to facilities. Prices vary considerably within each category and according to season. Always ask if a discount is applicable. Top-of-the-range *alberghi* **hotels** in Florence can be costly. However, there is plenty of fairly pricey mid-range and some budget accommodation. But do note that hotel rooms are very much in demand from Easter right through to autumn, so it's better to book as far in advance as possible.

The most convenient part of town to stay for sightseeing is the ***centro storico*** – all the city's sights are accessible by foot. For the privilege of staying in the historic heart of one of Europe's most beautiful cities, the price is high – and, as the centre is pedestrian-only, you are unlikely to be able to park your car nearby. Hotels along the banks of the **River Arno** are easier to reach though they also tend towards the pricey. Traditionally the area around **Sant Maria Novella** and the **railway station** was one for budget accommodation but there is now a good range of comfortable and luxurious hostelry here and you can park a car, or step from train to hotel. The addresses between **Santa Croce** and **San Marco** have risen in price, but the centre is minutes away and the area boasts plenty of trendy restaurants and cafés. Accommodation in the **suburbs** should be considered as it is less expensive, and bus transport is good.

Alternatives to Hotels
Agriturismo – rural accommodation – is a growing sector for tourism and offers accommodation of all standards in a country setting. The only snag here is that you will need a car for transport. For details, visit ⌨ www.agriturismo. regione.toscana.it
Pensioni – pensions – can be a good option as they are slightly smaller and intimate though some are positively luxurious being located in former palaces. At the bottom of the budget is a *Residenza*, which is even more basic but can be fine if you just want somewhere clean to sleep.

Centro Storico

• LUXURY
Savoy (Map C–D3)
A new look for the Savoy. This once-fading *risorgimento* building has been given a well-deserved glitzy facelift and has been renovated in sumptuous style. Piazza della Repubblica is a very fine central address.
✉ *piazza della Repubblica 7,*
☎ *055 27351,*
📠 *055 2735888,*
🖲 *reservations@ hotelsavoy.it*
💻 *www.hotelsavoy.it*

• MID-RANGE
Beacci Tornabuoni (Map C–C4)
A smart address for this excellent hotel, situated on Piazza Santa Trinità, at the lower end of via de' Tornabuoni. It is smallish but very well furnished.
✉ *via de' Tornabuoni 3,* ☎ *055 212645,*
📠 *055 283594,*
🖲 *info@bthotel.it*
💻 *www.bthotel.it*

Hotel Porta Rossa (Map C–C4)
An old-style hotel, with large, comfortable rooms, in the centre of town.
✉ *via Porta Rossa 19,*
☎ *055 287551,*
📠 *055 282179*

• BUDGET
Albergo Scoti (Map C–C4)
This small, cosy hotel is housed in a 15th-century palace. The bedrooms are simple, and the hotel is excellent value for its location. Pedestrian-only zone. Credit cards not accepted.
✉ *via de' Tornabuoni 7,* ☎/📠 *055 292128,*
🖲 *hotelscoti@ hotmail.com*

Hotel Dalí (Map C–F3)
A pleasantly furnished and quiet, small hotel located just behind the Duomo. Some of the rooms have views of the Duomo.
✉ *via dell'Oriuolo 17,*
☎/📠 *055 2340706,*
🖲 *hoteldali@tin.it,*
💻 *www.hoteldali.com*

Near the Arno

• LUXURY
Excelsior (Map C–A3)
Opulent, elegant and expensive, the Excelsior vies with the Grand opposite for its well-heeled custom. It affords great river views from the south-facing rooms.
✉ *piazza Ognissanti 3,*
☎ *055 264201,*
📠 *055 210278,*
🖲 *ExcelsiorFlorence@ westin.com*
💻 *www. luxurycollection.com/ excelsiorflorence*

Gallery Hotel Art (Map C–C5)
This hotel has been renovated and totally modernized into a very hip, zen-style establishment. Despite being so near the Ponte Vecchio, it is wonderfully tranquil.
✉ *vicolo dell'Oro 5,* ☎ *055 27263,*
📠 *055 268557,*
🖲 *bookings@ lungarnohotels.com*
💻 *www. lungarnohotels.com*

Grand

(Map B–E5)

This award-winning luxury hotel is situated directly opposite the Excelsior. It boasts richly decorated interior design, elegant rooms and suites. There are also good views from many of the rooms.

✉ *piazza Ognissanti 1,*
☎ *055 288781,*
📠 *055 217400,*
🖰 *GrandeFlorence@ luxurycollection.com*
🖥 *www. luxurycollection.com/ grandflorence*

Plaza Hotel Lucchesi (Map C–H6)

This is a beautiful, south-facing hotel with superb views towards Piazzale Michelangelo, just minutes from Ponte Vecchio. The best rooms overlook the Arno. Fine restaurant.

✉ *lungarno della Zecca Vecchia 38,*
☎ *055 26236,*
📠 *055 2480921,*
🖰 *phl@plazalucchesi.it*
🖥 *www. plazalucchesi.it*

• MID-RANGE

Hotel Goldoni

(Map C–A3)

Housed in an antique 18th-century palace, this comfortable hotel is just a few steps from the River Arno. Very central, it is conveniently situated for many of Florence's major attractions.

✉ *borgo Ognissanti 8,*
☎ *055 284080,*
📠 *055 282576,*
🖰 *info@ hotelgoldoni.com*
🖥 *www. hotelgoldoni.com*

Hotel River

(Map C–I6)

Not far from Santa Croce and overlooking the river, this is a comfortable hotel in the top end of the mid-range bracket. Ask for south-facing rooms for views of the River Arno.

✉ *lungarno della Zecca Vecchia 18,*
☎ *055 2343530,*
📠 *055 2343531,*
🖰 *info@ hotelriver.com*
🖥 *www. hotelriver.com*

Santa Maria Novella to San Lorenzo

• LUXURY

Hotel Londra

(Map B–E4)

Quiet, very comfortable modern hotel, with good restaurant. It has great views towards the southern Tuscan hills from the top-floor rooms. It is situated near the station and Santa Maria Novella church.

✉ *via Jacopo da Diacceto 16/20,*
☎ *055 27390,*
📠 *055 210682,*
🖰 *info@ hotellondra. com*
🖥 *www. hotellondra.com*

• MID-RANGE

Accademia

(Map C–C1)

A very comfortable, family-run *pensione* at the *centro storico* end of this long road.

✉ *via Faenza 7,*
☎ *055 293451,*
📠 *055 219771.*

Bellettini (Map C–C2)

A mid-sized hotel just a stone's throw from

the famous Medici Chapels. A comfortable address with all the monuments in the *centro storico* within easy walking distance.
✉ *via de' Conti 7,*
☎ *055 213561 or 282980,*
📠 *055 283551,*
📧 *hotel.bellettini@ dada.it*
💻 *www.firenze.net/ hotelbellettini*

Hotel Il Bargellino
(Map B–F4)
A moderately priced small hotel, family-run, with a fine terrace. Well-decorated rooms and appealing rooftop terrace, a little way out of the *centro storico*, but easily walkable.
✉ *via Guelfa 87,*
☎ *055 2382658,*
📠 *055 2382698,*
📧 *carmel@ ililbargellino.com,*
💻 *www. ilbargellino.com*

Hotel Unicorno
(Map C–B3)
Located amid tempting antique shops, this is a simply decorated but well-equipped hotel with modernized rooms.
✉ *via dei Fossi 27,*
☎ *055 287313,*
📠 *055 268332,*
📧 *reservations@ hotelunicorno.com*
💻 *www. hotelunicorno.it*

• BUDGET
Azzi (Map B–F4)
This is as inexpensive as it gets in a Florentine *pensione*, considering its central location. Simple rooms and friendly owners. If it is full, the **Anna**, on the floor above, is owned by the same proprietor and has similar prices.
✉ *via Faenza 56,*
☎ *055 213806,*
📠 *055 213806,*
📧 *hotelazzi @ hotmail.com*

Hotel Casci
(Map C–E1)
A small hotel, centrally located and close to all museums and monuments.
✉ *via Cavour 13,*
☎ *055 211686,*
📠 *055 2396461,*
📧 *info@ hotelcasci.com*
💻 *www. hotelcasci.com*

Fiorentina
(Map C–B3)
Spacious rooms, a short walk from the station, River Arno or Via de' Tornabuoni.
✉ *via dei Fossi 12,*
☎ *055 219530,*
📠 *055 287105.*

Hotel Sampaoli
(Map B–F4)
In an old palace north of Via Guelfa, a very small hotel with surprisingly spacious rooms at rock bottom prices.
✉ *via San Gallo 14,*
☎ *055 284834,*
📠 *055 282448,*
📧 *info@ hotelsampaoli.it*
💻 *www. hotelsampaoli.it*

San Marco to Santa Croce
• LUXURY
Hotel J and J
(Map C–H3)
This hotel is no more than a 10-minute walk due east from the

centre, and located in a former convent. It has tastefully furnished rooms.
✉ via di Mezzo 20,
☎ 055 263121,
📠 055 240 282,
📧 jandj@venere.it
🖥 www.jandjhotel.com

Morandi alla Crocetta (Map C–G1)
In a former convent, just by the Museo Archeologico, this is a small and rather elegant hotel with comfortably sophisticated decoration.
✉ via Laura 50,
☎ 055 234474,
📠 055 2480954,
📧 welcome @hotelmorandi.it,
🖥 www.hotelmorandi.it

• **MID-RANGE**
Residenza Johlea I
(Map B–G4)
Same ownership as the better known Residenza Johanna I and Residenza Johanna II, with the same format. However, this newly opened mini-hotel is

even more comfortable and far more central. For this reason it is marginally more expensive. Credit cards are not accepted.
✉ via San Gallo 80,
☎ 055 4633292,
📠 055 4634552,
📧 johlea@johanna.it
🖥 www.johanna.it

Oltrarno
• **LUXURY**
Hotel Lungarno
(Map C–C5)
Recently renovated, this mid-sized hotel overlooking the river has large rooms (some with terraces) stylishly decorated with antique furnishings.
✉ borgo San Jacopo 14, ☎ 055 27261,
📠 055 268437,
📧 bookings@lungarnohotels.com
🖥 www.lungarnohotels.com/lungarno

• **MID-RANGE**
Pensione Annalena
(Map B–E6)
In old 15th-century palace, once belonging to Lorenzo the Magnificent's grand-

father. Now a traditional but very comfortable pension, this is a perennial favourite with returning guests.
✉ via Romana 34,
☎ 055 222402 or 229600,
📠 055 222403,
📧 annalena@hotelannalena.it
🖥 www.florence.ala.it/annalena

• **BUDGET**
La Scaletta
(Map C–C6)
Small and cosy, some rooms in this hotel overlook the Boboli Gardens. La Scaletta has a roof garden and an excellent value restaurant.
✉ via Guicciardini 13,
☎ 055 283028 or 214255,
📠 055 289562,
📧 info@lascaletta.com
🖥 www.lascaletta.com

Sorelle Bandini
(Map C–A6)
Located right on the Piazza Santo Spirito, This is a charming if rather faded hostel

with an old-fashioned atmosphere dating right back to the 1920s when it was founded. Credit cards are not accepted.

✉ piazza Santo Spirito 9,
☎ 055 215308,
℡ 055 282761.

Further Afield

• LUXURY
Hotel Mirage
(Map B–A1)
Located just 20 minutes from the centre by regular bus, this is a comfortable hotel with a restaurant and parking. It is an ideal option for visitors with their own cars. Parking is free of charge.

✉ via F. Baracca 231/18, ☎ 055 352011,
℡ 055 374096,
✆ info@hotelmirage.it
🖳 www.hotelmirage.it

Villa La Massa
(Map A–G2)
A very luxurious small hotel located in a fine 16th-century building just 5km (3 miles) from the centre of Florence (at the start of the road to Pontassieve). It offers a great combination of a peaceful rural setting and proximity to the city.

✉ via della Massa 24, Bagno a Ripoli,
☎ 055 62611,
℡ 055 633102,
✆ lamassa@relaischateaux.fr
🖳 www.relaischateaux.fr

Villa San Michele
(Map A–G2)
This is the premiere choice for the romantic and the well-heeled. This former 16th-century convent turned luxury hotel offers the tranquillity of a rural position (and great views towards Florence) but manages to combine it with a supreme sense of elegance.

✉ via Doccia 4, Fiesole,
☎ 055 59451,
℡ 055 598734,
✆ reservations@villasanmichele.orientexpress.com
🖳 www.villasanmichele.oreintexpress.com

• BUDGET
Residenza Johanna I
(Map B–G3)
A very comfortable place to stay, located in a residential suburb north of the centre. Excellent value. Transport to the centre is just a short walk away. Credit cards not accepted.

✉ via B Lupi 14,
☎ 055 481896,
℡ 055 482721,
✆ info@johanna.it
🖳 www.johanna.it

Residenza Johanna II
(Map B–F3)
A sister residence to the Residenza Johanna I, this residence is located in a pleasant villa and has its own garden. It offers excellent value for money. Transport to the centre is just a short walk away. Credit cards are not accepted.

✉ via delle Cinque Giornate 12,
☎ 055 473377.

EATING OUT
What to Eat

Although the French might disagree, the Tuscans consider their cuisine amongst the world's finest. The region produces **excellent ingredients**: fresh fruit and vegetables, meat and fish. Combined with its fragrant herbs and some of the country's rich **olive oils**, its best wines and a small *digestivo*, this can add up to a simple and delicious cuisine.

Once seated at a table and after ordering from an à la carte menu, the waiter may well bring something to nibble on while you're waiting – *crostini*, small slices of baguette-type bread spread with liver pâté; *bruschetta*, large slices of bread rubbed in oil and salt; *grissini*, breadsticks, and slices of salt-free country bread.

The *primo piatto*, or first course, can take various forms. A *minestra*, soup, is a warm welcome in winter; try for instance the famous *acquacotta*, a bouillon vegetable soup with an egg on top, or *ribollita*, a well-stewed vegetable and bean soup. *Antipasto Misto*, mixed cold hors d'œuvres, is another favourite and might include Parma ham, salami, anchovies, artichoke, cooked mushrooms and sometimes cooked seafood.

The **pasta course** (in smart restaurants both *antipasto* and pasta are offered) will comprise plenty of familiar pastas. But it will often include, especially in winter,

polenta – originally a cornmeal staple of the poor, and an acquired taste. It is the **sauces** that change. There are always *ragù*, *bolognese*, minced meat with tomatoes; butter and sage sauces; basil-loaded pestos; and plain tomato, but try the *ragù de lepre*, made from hare and usually served with *pappardelle*, broad ribbon pasta; sauces made with cream and *rucola*, rocket; with *porcini* mushrooms or with *tartufo* (truffle – expensive but delicious). There is usually lasagna too.

When it comes to the *secondo piatto*, or main dish, there is nothing finer for the meat lover than the famous *bistecca alla Fiorentina*, a doorstep of rump steak, often grilled over an open fire, which should be prepared with Val di Chiana beef. Alternatively, *stracotto*, beef simmered in red wine, is excellent. *Vitello*, veal, comes in many guises: cold with a tuna sauce (odd but good), *scaloppine*, scallops, or *testina di vitello*, cooked veal head. *Agnello*, lamb, is particularly popular in spring while *lepre*, hare, *cinghiale*, boar, and other game are served in winter. Tripe and *coniglio*, rabbit, are served year-round, while poultry lovers should try *faraone*, guinea fowl, or *quaglia*, quail. *Pesce*, fish, and *frutti di mare*, seafood, though expensive, are both popular on the coast where nothing beats the delicious *fritto misto*, a light, easily digested presentation of mixed fried seafoods. Also look out for

Above: *For much of the year, one can eat outside in Florence. Here lingering lunchers enjoy the afternoon sun in Piazza della Signoria.*
Opposite: *The fertile hills of Tuscany produce myriad oils, wheat, olives and of course, Chianti wine.*

tonno, tuna, **pesce spada**, swordfish, and *sogliola*, sole, on menus.

Meat dishes are never served with **vegetables** – this comes extra: *spinaci*, spinach, *finocchi*, artichoke, *melanzane*, eggplant, *peperoni*, bell peppers, *fagioli*, white beans, or *fagiolini*, green string beans, and, in season, *fiori di zucchini*, courgette flowers, or *piselli*, peas. *Insalata mista*, mixed salad, is available everywhere.

Cheeses

Tuscany produces a few **formaggi**, cheeses, and its **pecorino** is perhaps the best of the lot. A mature sheep's milk cheese (sometimes with a percentage of cow's milk), it is served alone, on pasta, with pears or apples, and is quite delicious. Otherwise, restaurants offer a selection of Italy's best known cheeses such as Gorgonzola, Cacciacavallo, Dolcelatte, Parmigiano and Grana.

Desserts

These are not Italy's forte but you will find *tiramisù*, that creamy mascarpone, sponge and liquor confection that has travelled well beyond Italy's borders, and often baked and caramelized fruits. Siena produces **panforte**, a rich fruit cake. Throughout the year there are seasonal fruits which, in summer, can include figs, peaches, nectarines, strawberries (often with lemon juice), cherries and apricots. Alternatively, a Tuscan favourite is to take a glass of **vino santo**, a fine dessert wine somewhere between port and sherry. Enjoy it with **cantucci**, small, dry and very hard biscuits made with almonds which, when dipped in the wine, soften and melt in the mouth. As a parting thought, Perugia is known for its **Baci di Perugia**, or 'Perugian kisses' – a fine name for small chocolates and these can be found, packaged, in many good cafés and provision stores.

Stepping aside from fine cuisine, Tuscany also produces many a good **pizza**. Cooked in wood-fire ovens, they are a simple and filling alternative to *alta cucina*.

Ice Cream
Modern Italians think they invented **gelati** (they didn't – the Saracens in Sicily did by blending Etna's icy snow with local citrus) and thanks to its proliferation, have become the acknowledged masters of the creamy and sorbet type ices. It's a hot debate where the best ices come from, but Florence is among the winners. **Vivoli**, ✉ via Isola delle Stinche 7r, ☎ 055 292334, has consistently been among the best.

Wines and Spirits
The **wine** industry in Italy has expanded beyond all imagination in the last 30 years when the familiar Chianti bottle, the *fiasco*, was practically all anyone knew of Tuscan wine. There were even better wines, but they rarely left the country. Today, the **DOC** (*Denominazione di Origine Controllata*, the system of controlling the origin and the vinification of wine) and the superior **DOCG** (which adds that the quality is guaranteed) systems ensure a consistently good wine and the choice is vast. If you don't want to order a full bottle of wine, ask for *vino della casa*, house wine, which is usually sold by the quarter, half or litre.

Among the region's best wines are still its **Chianti Classico**, controlled more rigidly than before and therefore now of a higher quality than that from the Sienese and Florentine vineyards on the slopes of the Chianti hills; **Brunello di Montalcino** is one of the country's most reputed red wines and improves with ageing; **Vernaccia**, from San Gimignano, is a pale, dry wine; another white wine is the delicate **Bianco di Pitigliano**. Back with the reds, the **Nobile di Montepulciano** is also an excellent wine, and one for laying down.

Elba produces a rich, ruby-coloured **Dolce Aleatico**, a sweet red dessert wine, while the region's much loved *vino santo*, a straw-coloured or deep amber-hued dessert wine, is particularly appreciated from the Chianti Classico and Montepulciano areas.

Italy is also renowned for a number of apéritifs and *digestifs* which are excellent. Right at the top of the list are the apéritif brands **Campari**, **Cinzano** and **Martini**, while *digestifs* **Fernet Branca**, made from herbs, **grappa**, a spirit made from grape must, **amaretto**, an almond flavoured *digestif*, and **sambuca**, an aniseed liqueur, are all popular. At party time or to jazz up an apéritif, Italy's answer to champagne, ***prosecco*** (remember **Asti Spumante**?), brings a bit of bubble to the occasion.

Beer lovers have a choice between **Peroni**, **Nastro Azzuro** and **Moretti** which will probably be served *alla spina* (draught) in the bar.

Lastly, although tap water is perfectly safe in Florence, most Italians prefer bottled **mineral water**. Ferrarelle, San Pellegrino and San Benedetto are some of the popular *frizzante*, or sparkling waters.

Where to Eat

In a region renowned for its cuisine, eating out is a pastime to which Tuscans will devote their wallets and their unstinting attention. There are some remarkably good, traditional restaurants but few are cheap.

Top of the range are the *Ristoranti*. They follow traditions and will offer both a good menu and an expansive wine list, but are the most expensive. The most ubiquitous are the *trattorie*, a more familiar restaurant but with the accent on good food rather than on an elegant ambience. Prices depend on location and clientele. Other alternatives include the *enoteche* (wine bars) which over the last decade have become fashionable places to eat, too. Trattorie are falling from fashion as the smart set gen up on their wines and eat small dishes of excellent local fare as an accompaniment. For less expensive options look at a *tavola calda* or a *pizzeria*, some of which sell take-away pizza slices. Note that many restaurants close in August, and at least 1–2 days a week.

Above: *A superb choice of fresh produce is on sale daily in Florence's Mercato Centrale.*

Coffee Culture

The *espresso (caffè)*, quick, short, and strong, usually is drunk standing at the bar. If you fancy just a dash of milk, ask for a *caffè macchiato*. A *caffè corretto* is a coffee with a tot of grappa spirit. The *cappuccino* is an espresso, topped by frothy milk and dusted off with chocolate powder while *caffè latte* is milky coffee without the froth. A drink that's half milk, half coffee, is a *caffè lungo con latte* which may well be served in a glass. *Caffè Americano*, an insipid brew, is often made with instant coffee.

Above: Penne arra-biate *and slithers of parmesan cheese: a Tuscan favourite.*

Restaurants

Florence bursts with places to eat – from simple bars where a local wine is served with a freshly made sandwich, through to smart Michelin-rated restaurants. In the evenings Florentines usually stop at a bar for an apéritif, then continue to a favourite *trattoria*. Many, how-ever, have a soft spot (especially on week-ends) for dining in the Tuscan countryside, and reservations are advisable. Indeed, reservations are advisable anywhere in Florence unless you plan on dining before the locals – they con-gregate from 20:00 onwards. The fashion-able areas for eating out have changed over the last decade. Santa Croce and Santo Spirito now host some of the really great places.

Centro Storico
• LUXURY
Ottorino

This is the place for a traditional Tuscan meal – fresh ingredi-ents, good wines and elegant service.
✉ *via dell'Oche 12/16r,* ☎ *055 215151.*

• MID-RANGE
La Cantinetta Antinori

Antinori's own wines (excellent) in smart *enoteca* ambience. Good Tuscan food served in the wine bar area or in a smarter venue on the first floor.
✉ *piazza Antinori 3,* ☎ *055 292234.*

Osteria N.1

Cosy atmosphere, good food and fine pastas.
✉ *via del Moro 18022,* ☎ *055 284897,* ⏰ *closed Sundays.*

Il Paiolo

Tuscan cuisine in this family-run, small and popular restaurant in good central location.
✉ *via del Corso 42r,* ☎ *055 2150191,* ⏰ *closed Sundays.*

Il Latini

Oozing ambience, located just off fash-ionable via della Vigna Nuova. Semi-set menu. Booking is essential or be prepared to queue.
✉ *via del Palchetti 6,* ☎ *055 210916.*

• BUDGET
Le Mossacce

Popular Tuscan fare served in this small, family-run *trattoria*.
✉ *via del Proconsolo 55r,* ☎ *055 294361.*

I' Parione

This restaurant serves a blend of traditional and modern cuisine, and offers some inexpensive dishes.
✉ *via del Parione 74,* ☎ *05 214005.*

Santa Maria Novella
• LUXURY
Sabatini

For decades THE address for fine din-ing in Florence. A traditional grand-style

restaurant with excellent wines.
✉ *via de' Panzani 9/a,*
☎ *055 211559.*

• MID-RANGE
Trattoria La Carabaccia

This family-run *trattoria* serves authentic local fare, located in a non-touristy part of town.
✉ *via Palazzuolo 190r,* ☎ *055 214782.*

Buca Lapi

Authentic *trattoria* (one of the oldest in the city) popular with locals. Range of Tuscan specialities.
✉ *via del Trebbio 1,* ☎ *055 213768.*

• BUDGET
Marione

Good local restaurant, popular with Florentines and serving value-for-money fare.
✉ *via della Spada 27r,* ☎ *055 214756.*

Trattoria Croce al Trebbio

An old yet consistently good *trattoria*; Florentine specialities and

wine tasting in cellar.
✉ *via Belle Donne 47–49r,* ☎ *055 287009.*

San Lorenzo
• BUDGET
Baccus

A modern ambience for a popular, easy-going restaurant. Note the pastas.
✉ *borgo Ognissanti 45r,* ☎ *055 283714.*

Nerbone

Next to Perini's charcuterie, this hard-to-beat café cum *trattoria* has been going since 1872. Open in the mornings only.
✉ *Mercato Centrale,* ☎ *055 219949.*

San Marco to Santa Croce
• LUXURY
Enoteca Pinchiorri

Courtyard dining. Arguably Florence's best address, certainly one of the more expensive. Beautifully served and presented. Haute Italian cuisine.
✉ *via Ghibellina 87,* ☎ *055 242777.*

Taverna del Bronzino

Near Piazza della Indipendenza. In a fine old palazzo, a smart restaurant well-known to Florentines. Good value, fine wines. It is also quite near to San Marco.
✉ *via delle Ruote 25/27r,* ☎ *055 495220.*

Osteria del Caffè Italiano

An excellent though small classical Tuscan menu served in an elegant surround. A fine wine menu. Reservations recommended. Close to Santa Croce.
✉ *via Isola delle Stinche 11/13r,* ☎ *055289 368.*

• MID-RANGE
Alle Murate

Open evenings only, this beautiful restaurant never fails to please. It is nearer luxury in price but it has a fine wine cellar that attracts the cognoscenti.
✉ *via Ghibellina 52r,* ☎ *055 240618.*

La Maremma

Near Santa Croce, a traditional Florentine restaurant with a good ambience.

✉ via Verdi 16r,
☎ 055 244615,
🕐 closed Wed.

Baldovino

Also situated near Santa Croce, this modern-style restaurant serves most types of Italian food and includes some excellent salads. It has a sister restaurant, Beccofino (see under Oltrarno).

✉ via di San Giuseppe 27r, ☎ 055 241773.

Osteria dei Benci

A modern atmosphere and good, creative foods. Often full so reservations are advisable. Don't miss the desserts.

✉ via de' Benci 13r,
☎ 055234 4923.

• BUDGET
Il Pizzaiuolo

This is THE place for pizzas, prepared in authentic Neapolitan style. Good variety.

✉ via de' Macci 113r,
☎ 055 241171.

Oltrarno
• LUXURY
Enoteca Pane e Vino

This restaurant is located close to Ponte alle Grazie. It offers a set menu or à la carte wines. It is always popular and despite its name, serves excellent Tuscan meals.

✉ via di San Niccolò 70, ☎ 055 2476956.

• MID-RANGE
Beccofino

A top-notch chef produces excellent Tuscan cuisine in contemporary surrounds. Eat either in the restaurant or in the popular wine bar. Bookings advisable.

✉ Piazza degli Scarlatti, ☎ 055 290076.

Ristorante Ricchi

Catering specifically for fish-lovers, this is a modern, specialist restaurant.

✉ piazza Santo Spirito 8r, ☎ 055 215864, 🕐 closed Sun.

Momoyama Sushi Bar

This restaurant has a high-tech Japanese ambience and serves good sushi. An ideal place to go for Sunday brunch.

✉ borgo San Frediano 10r, ☎ 055 291840, 🕐 closed Mon.

• BUDGET
Trattoria del Carmine

Inside-outside dining in reasonably priced restaurant. A wide choice of Tuscan food is available.

✉ piazza del Carmine 18r, ☎ 055 218601.

Osteria Santo Spirito

Good, wholesome Italian food at affordable prices. Outdoor seating available.

✉ piazza Santo Spirito 16r, ☎ 055238 2383.

Borgo Antico

This is a traditional trattoria that serves good Tuscan home cooking.

✉ piazza Santo Spirito 6r, ☎ 055 210437.

Further Afield

• LUXURY

Lo Strettoio

This restaurant is located in a beautiful 17th-century villa setting in rural Florence (due north of the Duomo), with excellent Tuscan dishes.
⊠ *via Serpiolli 7, Serpiolli,* ☎ *055 4250044.*

• MID-RANGE

Fuori Porta

On the way to San Miniato al Monte, this is an *enoteca* for the serious wine drinker (and those who want the sunset from San Miniato). Light dishes to accompany.
⊠ *via Monte alle Croci 10,* ☎ *055 2342483.*

• BUDGET

Da Ruggero

Delicious home cooking is served in this always popular *trattoria*. Bookings are advisable.
⊠ *via Senese 89r (Porta Romana),* ☎ *055 220542.*

Out of Town

• LUXURY

La Panacea del Bartonlini

A place with great views and fine Tuscan food, incorporating some innovative ideas.
⊠ *via dei Bosconi 58A, Fiesole,* ☎ *055 548932.*

Arnolfo

This well-respected restaurant is one of Tuscany's best. Reservations essential. There is a great view from the terrace and, to round off the experience, there are four guest rooms.
⊠ *via XX Settembre 50, Colle di Val d'Elsa,* ☎ *0577 920549.*

• MID-RANGE

Il Feriolo

In a lovely atmospheric medieval building, this is a traditional restaurant serving familiar Tuscan dishes and good pastas.
⊠ *via Faentina 32, on Rt 32, 15km south of Borgo San Lorenzo,* ☎ *055 548932.*

Antica Trattoria La Torre

Under a tower in the main square, a very popular local restaurant with a rustic ambience. Family-run and hearty.
⊠ *piazza del Commune, Castellina in Chianti,* ☎ *0577 740236.*

Osteria Le Logge

In the centre of Siena, this attractively decorated restaurant offers consistently good local cuisine.
⊠ *via del Porrione 33, Siena,* ☎ *0577 48013.*

• BUDGET

Antica Fiaschetteria

A small but popular place with locals. Good snacks and traditional Tuscan dishes.
⊠ *piazza Lippi 4, Prato,* ☎ *0574 41225.*

Trattoria La Torre

A small but popular restaurant, known for its consistently good solid Tuscan fare.
⊠ *via Salicitto 7, Siena,* ☎ *0577 287548.*

ENTERTAINMENT

Evening entertainment in Florence centres around strolling, dining and enjoying a drink (but not necessarily in that order). Restaurants are abundant, as are cafés and bars, but much of the most typical Italian socializing is done observing others doing similar activities. **Piazza della Signoria** is prime people-watching territory, as are Piazza della Repubblica and Piazza di Santa Croce. The evening *passegiata* is usually between via Porta Rossa and the Ponte Vecchio, with a pause on this ancient bridge to look up and down the Arno. As happens in many other cities, street sellers appear in the evening and pedal souvenirs, scarves, cheap jewellery and the usual inexpensive handbags.

Like many other parts of Europe, the summer heralds a season of festivals, music and dance. Florence has plenty of *estivale* dates and up-to-date information on these can be noted from www.firenze.net.it or from the tourist office's own website: www.firenze. tourismo.toscana.it. Further afield, Fiesole runs a dance or theatre season staging performances in its Roman theatre (information from the tourist office, *see* page 75 or 🖳 www.comune.fiesole.it), while Lucca hosts its Lucca Summer Festival with internationally renowned performers (information from the tourist office, *see* page 77 or 🖳 www.comune.lucca.it), while the nearby town of Montecatini (known for its thermal waters and fancy spa and located just 48km or 30 miles from Florence) also stages an annual programme of concerts (information available from the tourist office, ☎ 0572 772244, 🖂 0572 70109).

Drinks and Bites

Rivoire
✉ piazza della Signoria 5r,
☎ 055 214412

Gilli
✉ piazza della Repubblica 39,
☎ 055 2396310

Procacci
✉ via de' Tornabuoni 64r, ☎ 055 211656

Giacosa
✉ via Tornabuoni 83r,
☎ 055 2396226

Cantinetta Antinori
✉ piazza Antinori 3,
☎ 055 292234

Enoteca Baldovino
✉ via di San Giuseppe 18r, ☎ 055 2347220

Fuori Porta
✉ via Monte alle Croci 10, ☎ 055 2342483

Beccofino
✉ piazza degli Scarlattti 1r,
☎ 055 290076

Vivoli
✉ via Isola delle Stinche 7r,
☎ 055 292334

Coronas Café
✉ via dei Calzaiuoli 72r, ☎ 055 2396139

BARS, NIGHTCLUBS AND DISCOS

Drinks and Bites

For those who would like to *fare com' i Fiorentini* (do as the locals do), a number of addresses are well worth noting (*see* panel on page 70 for details). In the famous Piazza della Signoria, **Rivoire** is the smart place for people-watching. In the large Piazza della Repubblica, go to **Gilli**.

For a midday drink or a sublime snack, a good place to stop is **Procacci**. Although only open in the daytime, **Giacosa** is the place to buy the best cakes, pastries and coffee in town.

For a drink in one of the trendy wine bars, try **Cantinetta Antinori**, **Enoteca Baldovino**, **Fuori Porta** and **Beccofino**.

As an after-dinner treat, an ice cream is almost *de rigueur*. A long-time favourite place for this is **Vivoli**, though **Coronas Café** is arguably just as good.

Bars, Nightclubs and Discos

Florence has its share of bars and discos (*see* panel on this page for details). Popular bars include **Hemmingway**, which is open in the evenings – a venue which combines tea-room, cocktail and oyster bar. **Il Caffè** is an

Bars
Hemmingway
✉ piazza Piatellina 9r,
☎ 055 284781

Il Caffè
✉ piazza de' Pitti 9r,
☎ 055 2396241

La Dolce Vita
✉ Piazza del Carmine,
☎ 055 284595

La Torre Caffè
✉ lungarno Cellini 56r,
☎ 055 680643

The Old Stove
✉ via Pellicceria 2-4r,
☎ 055 284640

Lion's Fountain
✉ borgo degli Abizi
34r, ☎ 055 2344412

Below: *Old money gathers at Gilli for a morning coffee or an evening apéritif.*

old-style coffee bar, open from mornings, and **La Dolce Vita** is open evenings. **La Torre Caffè** is open practically round the clock, while the Irish **The Old Stove** (a very Italian exterior hiding an Irish interior) and the **Lion's Fountain** are both open till 02:30 and serve Irish beers and other expatriate needs.

For further entertainment, there are a number of nightclubs and discos (*see* panel on this page for details). These include (in alphabetical order) **Full Up**, a centrally located disco with a young crowd and **Hurricane Roxy**, with disco music and a DJ in the evenings. **Jazz Club** is more mellow, and offers good jazz.

Night owls will find **Loch Ness** a good place to continue a long night's fun, while **Loonees** is a large underground venue which is invariably good fun, especially if you go with a group.

Macaraná manages to turn a restaurant into a show after 23:00 and keeps the tempo alive until 04:00 with disco music. Another local spot is **Maramao**, while the very popular **Meccanò** is a high-tech disco, with different themes nightly, for the energetic. If you are young and female, then **Space Electronic** will prove fun for its disco and karaoke. Once a cinema, now an entertainment venue, **Universale** has also proved very popular with the well-heeled set, and **Yab** is a central disco bar with live music and dancing.

Newcomer to the city's night birds, **Rio Grande**, brings the vibrant sounds of Latin America to Florence. Although it is a little excentred (it's in the Cascine district) this Brazilian *churrascaria* (grill) with both live shows and disco music, has made its mark on the night scene.

Nightclubs and Discos
Full Up
✉ via della Vigna Vecchia 23-25r,
☎ 055 293006

Hurricane Roxy
✉ via il Prato 58r,
☎ 055 210399

Jazz Club
✉ via Nuova de' Caccini 3,
☎ 055 2479700

Loch Ness
✉ via de' Benci 19r, ◷ open till 05:00

Loonees
✉ via Porta Rossa 15,
☎ 055 212249

Macaraná
✉ via Faenza 4,
☎ 055 210298

Maramao
✉ via de' Macci 79r,
☎ 055 244341

Meccanò
✉ via degli Olmi 1,
☎ 055 331371

Space Electronic
✉ via Palazzzuolo 37,
☎ 055 293082

Universale
✉ via Pisana 77r, ⌨
www.universalefirenze.it

Yab
✉ via de' Sassetti 5r,
☎ 055 215160

Left: *Although a second division player, Fiorentina still pulls in the local* tifosi *(fans)*.

Spectator Sports

Fiorentina is the city's football club. Currently a second division player with the familiar red lily on white emblem, their home grounds are at the **Stadio Comunale** (also known as Artemio Franchi), Viale Manfredo Fanti. For fixtures and information (in Italian) contact ✉ Piazza Savonarola 6, ☎ 055 50721, ⌨ www.fiorentina.it

Cinemas, Concerts and Theatres

On a more traditional note, Florence has good cinemas and theatres (*see* panel on this page for details). Original language films are on show at **Cinema Goldoni**, the **Instituto Frances** and the **Odeon**. Each May and June, the *Maggio Musicale*, a festival of classical music, is organized. For information, contact **Teatro del Maggio Musicale Fiorentino**. The **Teatro Comunale** hosts classical music and opera, as well as the *Maggio Musicale*. **Teatro della Pergola** is the venue for theatre and for music concerts organized by the **Amici della Musica**.

Cinemas and Theatres

Cinema Goldoni
✉ via dei Serragli 1,
☎ 055 222437

Instituto Frances
✉ piazza Ognissanti 2,
☎ 055 2398902

Odeon
✉ via de' Sassetti 1,
☎ 055 288488

Teatro del Maggio Musicale Fiorentino
✉ corso Italia 12,
☎ 055 211158,
⌨ www.maggiofiorentino.com

Teatro Comunale
✉ corso Italia 16,
☎ 055 211158 (for tickets and information)

Teatro della Pergola
✉ via della Pergola 12,
☎ 055 2264316,
📠 055 2264350,
⌨ www.firenze.net

Amici della Musica
✉ via G Sirtori 49,
☎ 055 608420,
⌨ www.amicimusica.fi.it

Orchestra da Camera Fiorentina
✉ via Poggi 6,
☎ 055 783374,
⌨ www.orcafi.it

Above: *The small town of Panzano rises above its neat Chianti vineyards.*

Getting Out of Town
Regular buses connect Florence to the major towns of Tuscany (see page 88 for details) while the rail services also connect Florence with Pisa, Arezzo and Siena (see page 88 for details). Half day and full day tours are also available from Florence with SITA (see page 87 for contact details). For those who want to take a leisurely route through Tuscany, car hire is recommended. For the best rates, organize and pay for this through one of the major car rental companies before leaving home Check out their websites for deals and local addresses:
⌨ www.hertz.com
⌨ www.budget.com
⌨ www.avis.com.

EXCURSIONS

There can hardly be a city in the world that has so many possibilities for excursions, be they of a half-day, full-day or a few days' duration. The Tuscan hills are full of historical towns but also countless areas of natural beauty. And beyond these, there is the Mediterranean coast.

A selection of a few of the major excursions are mentioned in the following pages. These include **Fiesole** which rises above Florence and presents the visitor, weather permitting, with a fine panorama of the city. It also boasts a rich past and some interesting monuments. **Prato**, formerly an individual small town, is now not only part of the urban development around Florence but also a provincial capital. Further west, the cities of **Pisa** and **Lucca** are world renowned. If you are travelling to and from Florence by plane, then Pisa can easily be combined with that journey. To the south, the charming town of **San Gimignano** is known for its Medieval towers. **Siena**, once a capital as powerful as Florence, could be a destination alone. Reserve it a fair share of your time. **Arezzo** is further afield, though accessible in a day from Florence. Its forte is the superb work by Piero della Francesca in one of its churches. And, if you are travelling by car, then venture into **wine country** and not only sample some of its superb wines, but discover some of Tuscany's small towns too.

Fiesole

It is only 8km (5 miles) to Fiesole but the attractive small town situated on the top of a hill has its own special atmosphere and was much appreciated by the 19th-century travellers; the popular film, *A Room with a View*, was set here.

The views are, indeed, what bring most visitors to the town (or beyond in the area's delightful rural roads) and from the large, sloping **Piazza Mino da Fiesole** (a tribute to the local sculptor), Florence fans out in the mid-distance. This is the centre of town, a touristy area in which cafés and vendors capitalize on foreign trade and Florentines out for a weekend excursion, but the nearby **Duomo** offers a peaceful respite and hosts two tombs by Mino da Fiesole.

It would also be a shame to miss the massive Etruscan walls or the well-preserved Roman Theatre in the **Zona Archeologica** (open daily, except the first Monday of the month). These are just five minutes' walk from the piazza. The **Museo Archeologico** displays some exceptional Etruscan statues and other finds from the Zona.

All art enthusiasts ought to make the effort to visit **San Domenico di Fiesole** (between Fiesole and Florence). This is the church where **Fra Angelico** took his vows, and is home to his 1430 painting of the *Virgin, Saints and Angels*.

Fiesole
Location: Map A–G2
Distance from Florence: 8km (5 miles)
✉ Tourist Office: APT, piazza Mino da Fiesole 35
☎ 055 598720
📠 055 598822
💻 www.firenze.turismo.toscana.it
🍽 Restaurants around Piazza Mino da Fiesole.

Below: *Hidden from prying eyes by the ubiquitous cypress trees, luxurious villas are sited in the hills around Fiesole, many turned southwards with expansive views towards Florence.*

Prato

A Medieval oasis in the midst of an ugly industrial landscape, old Prato is fascinating and easily accessible from Florence for a half-day trip. For centuries it has been renowned for its wool cloth, and the town's rich merchants erected fine buildings. Nowadays it is better known for its modern factories and light industry.

The first stop should be the **Duomo**, in the heart of town, resplendent with **Filippo Lippi's** fresco cycle of the *Life of St John* and the *Life of St Stephen*, and an elegant synthesis of early Romanesque and later Gothic styles. The **Chapel of the Holy Girdle** houses the Virgin's famous girdle relic; it is brought out into public five times a year. On leaving, look up the external pulpit created by architect and sculptor **Michelozzo**. It is an unusual and stunning piece of work. The original pulpit panels, crafted by **Donatello**, are now in the **Museo dell' Opera del Duomo**. A few minutes away, in Piazza del Commune, is the rather forbidding 13th-century **Palazzo Pretorio**. Another structure worth seeing, and from the same era, is the **Castello dell'Imperatore**, situated next to the Renaissance **Santa Maria delle Carceri**.

Prato
Location: Map A–G2
Distance from Florence: 18km (11 miles)
✉ Tourist Office: APT, via Cairoli 48
☎ 0574 24112
📠 0574 24112
🖥 www.firenze.turismo.toscana.it
🍴 Restaurants near Piazza Lippi.

Below: *Prato's unusual external pulpit, designed by Michelozzo, originally held panels by Donatello.*

Lucca

Fortified by its now-grassy ramparts and bastions, Lucca rose to prosperity and power in the Middle Ages, becoming a city state during the Renaissance. It still retains much of its **Medieval** and **Renaissance** ambience thanks to its political stability over the centuries. Its architecture is very distinctive and despite its being a mid-sized city, its *centro storico* is easy to explore by foot.

The oldest extant Romanesque church in Lucca, **San Michele in Foro**, in the piazza of the same name, was built on the remains of the Roman Forum. Its unusual façade is capped by a powerful statue of Archangel Michael, wings open, flanked by two smaller angels. Just a couple of metres down Via di Poggio is the **Casa Natale di Puccini**, birthplace of the Italian composer.

The old bastions are still in evidence, and make a fine walk. Go to the **Baluarte San Frediano** and visit the nearby church of San Frediano, with its glittering 13th-century mosaic. It's best in the early morning sun.

In the lovely **Piazza San Martino**, surrounded by a potpourri of buildings, lies the town's **Duomo**, the cathedral dedicated to St Martin. Its Medieval **campanile** towers over the terracotta roofs of the *centro storico*. Laboriously carved Romanesque sculpture, in a good state of conservation, decorate this asymmetrical western front. Inside the rather gloomy cathedral are the much-venerated crucifix, the **Volto Santo**, which is said to have been begun by Nicodemus; and Jacopo della Quercia's richly decorated white marble tomb of **Ilaria del Carretto Guinigi**, wife of one of the town's wealthy 15th-century rulers.

Above: *A statue of composer Giacomo Puccini, Lucca's favourite son.*

Lucca
Location: Map A–E2
Distance from Florence: 79km (49 miles)
✉ Tourist Office: APT, Vecchia Porta San Donato/Piazzale Verdi
☎ 0583 419689
📠 0583 312581
🍽 There are restaurants around Piazza San Michele in Foro, Piazza dell'Anfiteatro and also around Via Roma.

Above: *Torre Pendente – the famous Leaning Tower of Pisa.*

Pisa

Centuries ago, Pisa was on the sea but subsequent silting of the River Arno cut off the city's maritime links more effectively than any invader. It gained its independence in the 9th century and expanded trading links during the Middle Ages. At its height, Pisa rivalled both Venice and Genoa. It was also home to **Galileo Galilei**.

Pisa's **Torre Pendente** never fails to thrill. Its anchoring section of blind arcades, surmounted by the familiar six tiers of shallow arcades and capped by its bell tower, are all immediately recognizable. The tower is now 5m (16ft) off-centre (it started inclining even as it was being constructed by its architect, **Bonanno Pisano**, in 1173) but recent remedial work has stabilized it and it is, once again, open to tourists.

For visitors, however, the delightful **Battistero** is almost more appealing. Directly beyond the west front of the **Duomo**, the round Baptistry was begun in 1153 but not finished for nearly 250 years. Recalling a regal headdress in shape, it is totally unique in style. Pride of place is the magnificent and elaborate pulpit by **Nicola Pisano**. Signed and dated 1260, this hexagonal masterpiece comprises six panels sculpted in bold relief, depicting five scenes from the New Testament.

Lastly, take time to visit the **Camposanto**. Once a cemetery, it houses some exquisite pieces of Roman sculpture and sarcophagi.

Pisa
Location: Map A–D3
Distance from
Florence: 82km
(51 miles)
✉ Tourist Office: APT, via Carlo Cammeo 2
☎ 050 560464
📠 050 42291
🖥 www.firenze. turismo.toscana.it
🍽 Restaurants around Via Carducci and Via Roma.

San Gimignano

Long before you arrive at San Gimignano you'll see its 14 famous **towers**. There were once 72 of them – they were constructed by rival Guelfs and Ghibellines to protect themselves from opposing factions.

Tourism has unfortunately discovered this appealing small town so visitors should park cars outside, and take a leisurely stroll through its ancient walls, to discover its monuments, cafés and restaurants, not forgetting the many souvenir shops selling local Vernaccia wines, pottery and decoratively packaged foodstuffs.

Top sights include the **frescoes** of Santa Fina, in the **Collegiata di Santa Maria Assunta**, once the cathedral. This austere, 12th-century Romanesque building was enlarged in the 1460s by architect and sculptor, Giuliano da Maiano. The **Cappella di Santa Fina** was decorated by Domenico Ghirlandaio.

Passing by the late 13th-century **Palazzo Popolo**, which encloses the **Museo Civico**, an alley leads to the **Piazza della Cisterna**, named for the well in its centre, a pretty piazza paved in brick (like nearby Piazza Pecori) laid out in a traditional herringbone design. Don't miss the **Benozzo Gozzoli frescoes** in San Agostino, a renovated church in the peaceful Piazza San Agostino, at the northern side of town.

Like its inhabitants, you can stroll late in the afternoon from San Gimignano (the countryside is pretty) and pause to look at the town's unique profile.

San Gimignano
Location: Map A–F4
Distance from Florence: 77km (49 miles)
⊠ Tourist Office: APT, Piazza Duomo 1
☎ 0577 940008
✆ 0577 940903
🖳 www.firenze.turismo.toscana.it
🍴 There are restaurants around Piazza della Cisterna and off Via San Matteo.

Below: San Gimignano once boasted over 70 towers. Today some 14 still stand.

The Hermit and the Ensign
At via delle Cerchia 50–52 is an ancient marble head of a hermit with a story to tell. In war-torn 1207 a young hermit had a dream in which his patron saint, Andrew, urged him to help the Sienese cause. He followed the military from the Porta all'Arco into battle under their white banner. The next day he was found dead splayed across the white flag which, soaked in blood, had turned red. Not all the flag was bloodied: a diagonal cross stayed white. The cross of St Andrew – a white transversal cross on red – was henceforth adopted as their military insignia.

Siena

Possibly another Etruscan settlement that was appropriated by the Romans, Sena Julia was, however, confirmed as a Roman colony in 1BC. It stagnated until the early Middle Ages when its trade expanded into northern Europe, and it gained a reputation, and considerable wealth, as a banking centre. Its money lenders soon put it on a par with Florence. However, this similarity degenerated into rivalry as Florence became Guelf, and Siena, Ghibelline. Despite the battles, the 12th and 13th centuries constituted the period of greatest prosperity, economic and artistic, for this powerful town and many of its characteristic brick buildings date from this period.

The **Piazza del Campo**, Siena's medieval heart, is probably Italy's most attractive piazza and certainly one of its more unusual. Shaped like an open fan, it is divided by white stone 'spokes' into nine brick-paved sections, to recall the **Council of Nine**. Medieval buildings line its perimeter, facing inwards and down the sloping piazza to the magnificent **Palazzo del Pubblico** at the lower end – a building crowned by its impossibly thin **Torre del Mangia**. Favourite venue for the evening *passegiata* and affluent café-goers, the piazza turns into a wild frenzy for the bi-annual **Palio** when 30,000 people cram into its centre as the horse-back riding competitors from 10 of the 17 *contrade* battle it out for 30 crucial seconds in a race around the piazza's perimeter. The ancient Palazzo del Pubblico now houses the **Museo Civico**, the city's best art museum, a priceless collection which outlines the history of Sienese art.

It is a few minutes' walk via the appropriately named **Via Pellegrini**, Pilgrims' Way, to the **Duomo**. This extraordinary white, green and pink-striped building, started in the 12th century, was to be incorporated into a far larger church designed in the mid-13th century, but these ideas were finally scrapped in favour of the original less grandiose plans, and it was finished 200 years later. Its roots were Romanesque (as is its striped **Campanile**) but much of its execution – those pointed and ogive arches, gabled doorways, pinnacles, and niches with sculpture – is Gothic. If you want to see the Duomo's treasures, then visit the **Museo dell'Opera del Duomo** where they are displayed.

Above: *Overshadowed by the Torre del Mangia, the Palazzo del Pubblico houses a fine collection of early Sienese art.*

Adjacent to the Duomo, the **Libreria Piccolomini** was constructed to house the library of Pope Pius II. Pinturrichio's fabulous fresco decoration is a colourful marvel.

Another interesting building is the **Ospedale di Santa Maria della Scala**, a 13th-century hospital built to house the Medieval pilgrims travelling via Siena to Rome. It ceased functioning as a medical facility in 1996. It has superb, restored frescoes depicting in a very graphic fashion, hospital life in the 15th century. It is located near the entrance to the cathedral.

For the keen, there are more churches to visit, but perhaps the strongest memories of Siena are those absorbed as one walks through its narrow, pedestrian streets, past old homes, smart shops and tiny restaurants, along thoroughfares that have hardly changed in 700 years.

Siena
Location: Map A–G4
Distance from Florence: 71km (44 miles)
✉ Tourist Office: APT, piazza del Campo 56
☎ 0577 280551
📠 0577 270676
🖥 www.firenze.turismo.toscana.it
🍽 Many restaurants around Piazza del Campo, Via del Porrione and Via del Castoro.

Above: *Arezzo's Piazza Grande has a medieval feel.*

Arezzo

Location: Map A–I4
Distance from Florence: 80km (50 miles)
✉ Tourist Office: APT, paizza della Repubblica 28
☎ 0575 377678
🖷 0575 20839
🖥 www.firenze. turismo.toscana.it
🍴 Restaurants off Corso Italia, Piazza Grande and Via Mazzini.

Arezzo

At first sight, Arezzo is not an attractive town. But its lovely old centre attests to its prosperous past, both in Etruscan and Renaissance times. Arezzo was also the birthplace of **Petrarch**, artist **Spinello Aretino** and architect **Giorgio Vasari**. But it is in fact better known for one of the most remarkable fresco cycles of the Renaissance: **Piero della Francesca's** *Legend of the True Cross*, worth the journey alone. This unique work is simply breathtaking and it's worth taking time to understand the various sections. Piero's depiction of the story, his scholarship in anatomy, mathematics and perspective, and his interest in depicting real characters were all groundbreaking at the time. Recently restored, this chapel gleams like a jewel.

The town's focal point is the **Piazza Grande**, a large, sloping piazza. It has a fine medieval feel thanks to its remaining crenellated towers, narrow, old houses and views of the lovely Romanesque **Santa Maria della Pieve**. The piazza is also home to the monthly **Antiques Fair**, and the riotous annual joust, **Giostra del Saracino**, held in late August or early September.

Santa Maria della Pieve is without doubt one of the most impressive Romanesque churches in Tuscany. The rounded apse with its delightful double-storey arcade, and its noble campanile, are excellent examples of this 12th-century style. The self-designed home of architect Vasari, in Via XX Settembre, is open to visitors, as is the dignified stone house once occupied by Petrarch, via dell'Orto 28, now the seat of the Petrarch Academy.

Wine Country

It is a pleasure to travel through the Chianti vineyards, interspersing sightseeing with wine tasting and fine local cuisine. The area is easily accessible for drivers from Florence.

At the heart of the Florentine Chianti region, **Greve in Chianti** is a leading centre for Chianti and a regional market town. The unusual triangular 'square', **Piazza Matteotti**, forms the heart of town.

On the hills either side of Greve are small country roads leading to some attractive villages and castles. Among these is the medieval **Montefioralle**, on the road to Tavarnelle Val di Pesa. Continue onward up and over the hill for another 6–7km (4 miles) and you'll come to the **Badia a Passignano**.

The **Via Chiantigiana** continues southwards to Siena, passing through **Castellina in Chianti**, a pleasant 13th-century walled town with an unusual vaulted street, Via delle Volte, which follows the contours of the town walls. Along with Radda and Gaiole, Castellina formed part of the *Lega di Chianti*, the **Chianti League**.

More sightseeing could take you to the monastic complex at Coltibuono, **La Badia a Coltibuono**, the town of **Gaiole in Chianti**, and further south to the castle at **Meleto** – a restored stronghold dating from the 12th century, which remains privately owned. The castle at **Brolio**, however, is open to visitors. This magnificent 15th-century castellated building is owned by the well-known noble family (and wine producer), Ricasoli.

Wine Country

Location: Map A

Distance from Florence: Greve in Chianti: 31km (20 miles); Castellina in Chianti: 61km (38 miles); Gaiole in Chianti: 60km (37 miles)

✉ Greve Tourist Office: APT, via Luca Cini 1

☎ 055 8545243

📠 055 8544654

💻 www.firenze.torismo.toscana.it

🍽 Restaurants include those in Piazza del Comune in Castellina, Via della Montagnola in Strada in Chianti, and Piazza Trieste in Greve.

Below: *Triangular Piazza Matteotti, in Greve in Chianti, is the social heart of this wine-producing town.*

Above: *The Duomo dominates this fine view over the centre of Florence.*

Best Times to Visit

Spring and autumn are the favourite times to visit Florence as the weather can be delightful, mild and often sunny – ideal for exploration on foot. Outside the city, the countryside is at its best in these seasons. Of course, summer is warmer and drier, but you have to share the city with many other tourists though the Italians, themselves, will often be on holiday during the month of August and some city restaurants may be closed. Winter is a good bet for those who don't mind the cool, sometimes rainy, weather, for the museums and churches are far less crowded.

Tourist Information

The Ente Nazionale Italiano per il Turismo (ENIT) is the publicity arm for promotion of Italy overseas, 🖥 www.enit.it. It can be contacted in the United Kingdom (London), the USA (New York, Chicago and Los Angeles) in Canada and in Australia, ✉ Level 26, 44 Market Street NSW 2000 Sydney, ☎ 02 92 621666, 📠 02 92 621677, 🖰 enitour@ihug.com.au. Within Tuscany, the Azienda di Promozione Turistica (APT) is the place to head for local tourist information, 🖥 www.firenze.tourismo.toscana.it. In Florence this is at ✉ via Cavour 1r, ☎ 055 290832, 📠 055 2760383 🖰 infoturismo@provincia.fi.it ✉ Piazza Stazione, (Railway Station), ☎ 055 212245 and ✉ Borgo Santo Croce 29r, ☎ 055 2340444, ◷ 90:00–19:00 Mon–Fri, 09:00–18:00 Sat, and 10:00–15:00 Sun and public holidays. Their rather decentralized head office is at ✉ via A. Manzoni 16, Florence, 📠 055 2346286, 🖥 www.firenze.tourismo.toscana.it Further information about Florence and her sights, sites, excursions and other practical information can be found at ⌨ www.firenze.net www.mega.it/florence www.firenze-web.it and www.fionline.it

Entry Requirements

Visitors with EU nationality require a valid national identity card or a passport, with minimum 6 months before expiration. All other visitors require a valid passport. Non EU citizens wishing to stay longer than 90 days will require a visa, as do some other nationals including South Africans, New Zealanders and Australians.

Customs

Custom regulations for EU citizens are 800 cigarettes, 200 cigars or 1kg (2.2lbs) tobacco; 10 litres spirits, 90 litres wine and 110 litres of beer. For non-EU nationals, the limits are 200 cigarettes or 100 cigars,

1 litre spirits or 2 litres fortified wine and two litres of wine.

Health Requirements

There are no special requirements for entry into Italy. The only health hazards might include the occasional upset stomach and perhaps excessive exposure to the summer sun. EU citizens qualify for free medical treatment on presentation of the appropriate form (the E111 for British citizens). Visitors from elsewhere should arrange their own travel and medical insurance.

Getting There

Florence is accessible by road, rail and air.
By air: There are two international airports in Tuscany serving Florence: Amerigo Vespucci, ☎ 055 30615), ✉ 4km (2.5 miles) northwest Florence. There are frequent taxi services from the airport to centre. Airlines serving

this airport include: Meridiana, Lufthansa and Air France. Pisa has a much bigger international airport (Galileo Galilei, ☎ 050 849401) ✉ just 3km (2 miles) south of Pisa and 75km (48 miles) from Florence. Hourly train services from Pisa airport connect with Florence, via the centre of Pisa. Airlines serving this airport include: Alitalia, British Airways, Go and Ryanair. For flight information contact Alitalia ☎ 055 27881 in Florence or ☎ 050 500707 in Pisa; and Meridiana ☎ 055 32961 in Florence.
By rail: The Ferrovie dello Stato, Italian State Railway network, spans over 16,000km (10,000 miles) linking in the north, the borders with France, Switzerland and Austria and onward via ferries to Sardinia, and Sicily in the south. First and second class rail tickets can be purchased at either stations or at travel

agents. Supplements are payable with the high-speed trains such as Eurostar (which runs an inter-city service between large cities in Italy and beyond its frontiers) and the slightly less expensive Inter-city and Euro-city. Otherwise there are regular Espressi, Diretti, Interregionali and Regionali each slower than the former and stopping at more stations. Foreigners can benefit from special travel tickets such as the Eurodomino (permitting 3, 5 or 10 full calendar day's travel, unlimited mileage within each specified day, for a month after the first date used), bought at railway stations on proof of foreign residency. Two main lines serve Tuscany: Turin-Genoa-Viareggio-Grosseto-Rome and the route Milan-Bologna-Florence-Arezzo-Rome. From Milan trains take just over 3 hours to Florence, and from Rome, 94 minutes. All tickets must be validated by a punchmark from a machine on or near the platform. Information in English can be obtained on the FS 🖳 www.fs-on-line.com.

By road: Italy has a good network of roads and motorways (*autostrade*), indicated by green sign posts. Florence is on the toll-paying Autostrada del Sole, the A1, which links Milan (298km or 186 miles from Florence) via Bologna (105km or 65 miles from Florence) and skirts Florence going on to Rome (277km or 173 miles) and Naples (496km or 310 miles). For ease, take the toll-paying autostrade, but for pleasure, stick to the *strade statali* (state roads), and the smaller bi-roads. Speed limits are 120 kph (75mph) on *autostrade*, 90 on state roads and 60 on urban roads. Seatbelts are compulsory as is the wearing of helmets for motorcyclists. All visitors arriving by private car or motor-bike must carry the vehicle's documents, their driving licence, and require valid insurance cover – the Green Card. Travellers entering Italy by road from northern Europe can do so on toll high-ways (*autostrade*) from France (via Ventimiglia), various passes and tunnels through the Alps from Switzerland and Austria and, skirting Milan, can continue south on the A1, the Autostrada del Sole to Florence. Eurolines run 3 weekly direct bus services between London (Victoria) and Florence, 🖳 www.eurolines.it or contact the local agents; ✉ Lazzi, via Paisiello 13r, Florence, ☎ 055 355305, 🖳 www.lazzi.it. Travel time is just under 16 hours. Information in the UK, on ☎ 0990 808080, in Italy call Lazzi, ☎ 055 355305.

For bus services to other Italian cities, contact CAP, ✉ largo Fratelli Alinari 9, Florence, ☎ 055 214637; ✉ Lazzi, via Paisiello 13r, Florence, ☎ 055 355305, 🖥 www.lazzi.it; SITA, ✉ via Santa Caterina da Siena 15, Florence, ☎ 055 214721.

What to Pack

During the winter months, bring warm clothing, a collapsible umbrella and a raincoat or light rain jacket. Inexpensive hotels are not always well heated so bring warm bedwear and an extra pair of socks. Spring and autumn days can be either cool or warm so layered clothing is best. A showerproof jacket is useful. Summer clothing should be light with a jacket or woollen for evenings. Most restaurants, except the most exclusive, do not require tie and jacket but since Florentines love dressing up, you'll feel more comfortable making a bit of a sartorial effort.

For the lovers of art history, comfortable shoes are a must while binoculars aid appreciation of poorly lit ceilings. Pack a separate purse for the ever-necessary change required to light up chapels and churches.

Money Matters

Italy's currency is now the Euro, shared with 11 other countries of the European Monetary Union. There are many banks and exchange bureaux (*cambio*) but most visitors find the easiest way of obtaining currency is an Automatic Teller Machine (ATM), called a *Bancomat* in Italy, with a credit card (Visa, Mastercard etc) and your pin number. In most cases, the credit card operator will levy a fee for the transaction, as will the bank or *cambio*. Italian sales tax is called IVA. It is currently at 20% and is

---

Map it Out

Can't find an address on a map? Don't know at which end of a long street it is located? Computer users might want to log onto 🖥 www.maporama.com and fill in the street address and city. After a short wait you will be given a street plan with the address correctly identified.

Road Signs

Senso unico • One-way street

Alto • Stop

Avanti • Go (on a pedestrian crossing)

Sottopassaggio • Pedestrian underpass

Passo carribile • Don't park here – the entrance is constantly in use

Benzina • Petrol/gas

Fermata • Bus stop

Uscita • Exit

Questura • Police station

Autostrada • Motorway

Pedaggio • Toll

Accendere i fari • Turn your lights on

Curva molto pericolosa • Very dangerous bend

ATAF Tickets

A new cooperation between bus services now enables a passenger to buy his ATAF ticket (from the one-hour type to the one-month season ticket) and use any of the city buses plying his route. He may also change buses and bus service providers within the given time framework of his ticket.

not always included in the price of an article. Also note that some restaurants add both sales tax and a hefty service tax onto bills. Tipping is still optional though Italians will usually round up a figure or leave up to 10% for excellent service.

Transport

Once in Florence, the best way to get around is to walk; the *centro storico* is pedestrian-only, but it is compact. If you are lodging further away, metered white taxis (*see below*) are available. Most cab drivers can speak sufficient English to understand a destination. Four electric-powered town buses ply the streets. The railway station is the terminus for two of these bus lines. Tickets for single journeys, valid one hour each, to be bought in advance from *tabacchi*, kiosks selling newspapers, shops displaying the

New Cab System

In a bid to reduce traffic congestion, Florence has introduced a new system for some of its taxis. Nearly 600 cabs are licenced to offer a multiple service, that is to pick up two or more people travelling independently along the same given route. Taxis are colour coded for the major cross-city routes and they can be flagged down on these routes and the cost of the ride shared by participating passengers.

ATAF sticker, or the station. Women travellers should take the usual precautions when travelling alone at night – or take a metered taxi from the destination to the hotel. Bike enthusiasts can rent bikes through Florence by Bike, ✉ via San Zanobia 120r/122r, ☎ 055 488992. Taxis are available on ☎ 055 4242, 055 4390 and 055 4798. For travelling further afield, there is an excellent network of roads radiating out from Florence. From Florence's Railway Station there are buses to many destinations. For Instance, the No. 7 goes to Fiesole while Prato is on the main Milan–Rome railway line. Another line runs from Florence to Viareggio, via Pistoia, and Lucca. There are regular trains between Florence and Siena, a journey time of 94 minutes and buses run into Siena's city centre. Arezzo is on the main Milan to Rome railway line and takes 30–80 minutes from Florence (depending of type of train), and 90–120 minutes from Rome. Other towns are not so easy to access with public transport. But for those who are visiting Florence without their own transport, renting a car (Hertz, Budget or Avis) is easy at the airports or from the centre of Florence. Do not leave your valuables or possessions visible in cars.

Business Hours

Food shops and markets ⏰ 07:30, closing for lunch around 12:30–13:00. Shops reopen in the afternoon at 16:00–19:00 or later. Fashion stores, open Mon–Sat and rarely open before 10:30. Some close for lunch. Others remain open until 19:00–20:00.

Banks: Banks ⏰ Mon–Fri, 08:30–13:30 and again 14:30–15:30. They are closed at weekends. They also close earlier in the morning the day prior to a public holiday.

Museums and Monuments: There are many variants but as a very broad generalization, ⏰ 09:00–19:00, with a 2-hour lunch break, Tue–Sat, and 09:00–13:00 on Sun. Some private galleries operate different hours and close weekly on a day other than Mon. Most have different timetables from winter to summer. Few (although there are some) open on public holidays. It is wise, perhaps, to telephone the relevant tourist office to ascertain opening hours if you particularly want to see a specific museum or monument.

Churches: These open early morning, ⏰ 7:00 and will close at 18:00. Many churches will close over lunchtime between 12:00 and 16:00.

Time Difference

Italy's time is GMT + 1 hour in winter, and GMT + 2 from the last Sunday in March to the last Sunday in October in summer. The 24-hour clock is used in Italy.

Communications

Post: Mail from Italy can be slow with the exception of the new 24-hour delivery service (at a premium price). Stamps for postcards and light letters can be bought from *tabacchi*, tobacconists who are open longer hours than *La Posta*, the post office. For packages and other mail, go to the *Ufficio Postale Centrale*, Main Post Office, in Florence, ✉ via Pellicceria 3, ⏰ Mon–Fri 08:30–13:20; on Sat it closes at 12:00.

Telephones: Public phones are operated by both coins or increasingly, prepaid *schede* or *carte telefoniche*, telephone cards (available from newsstands, post offices or *tabacchi*). Some telephone cabins accept international credit cards and others can even send faxes. Mobile phones operate on 1800 and 900 MHZ frequencies, with comprehensive coverage. All numbers in Italy start with a '0' unless they are free phone numbers. Unlike the practices in some other countries, you must always dial the '0' and the code whether or not you are in the same town and whether or not you are overseas.

Faxes: These can be sent from the post office, and also from a number of cabins around town.

Internet: In Florence, Siena, Pisa and Lucca there are plenty of inexpensive cyberspaces for e-mail and surfing the Net.

Electricity

The current in Italy is 220V AC and Italian plugs are two pin, round ones. Adapters are available in electrical stores in most countries (or at large airports on departure) while American visitors will need a transformer to use 110V appliances.

Weights and Measures

Italy follows the metric system. When buying food in delis, cold meats etc. are often sold by the *etto*, 100g (3.4oz) units.

Health Precautions

There are no particular health warnings for tourists in Florence. The tap water is safe, if not particularly pleasant but bottled mineral water is widely available. In summer, bring sun screen and mosquito repellent. Medical facilities are good in Italy but inevitably expensive. Take out medical insurance for your trip or if you are an EU citizen, make sure you get an E111 form. For minor problems ask a pharmacist for advice. For urgent first aid, *pronto soccorso*, go to the outpatients department of the local hospital. Alternatively dial **113** for an emergency.

Personal Safety

Petty theft is Italy's main drawback. Bag snatching and pickpocketing is rife in tourist areas and on crowded buses and trains during peak travel times. It is a good idea to carry cash and credit cards in a money belt. Be aware at all times. We suggest carrying a photocopy of your passport in your wallet and leaving the passport along with air tickets and other valuables in safe keeping at your hotel. Single women travellers should be especially vigilent and careful about walking around town alone late at night. Italians are notorious for staring at attractive women, even passing the odd comment but most of it is not malicious, and certainly not a real source of sexual harassment. If driving around Tuscany, you will sometimes have to leave your car quite far from hotel or sights so do not leave anything visible inside the car.

Emergencies

If you are robbed, report the incidence immediately to the *Carabinieri* (military police) at their *caserma*, or to the *polizia* (civil police) at the *questura*, or telephone the emergency number, ☎ 113. For fire emergencies, ☎ 115 and for breakdown assistance on the road, ☎ 116. For medical assistance in English, ☎ 06 8080995 while for health emergencies, ☎ 118.

Etiquette

General politeness is still appreciated and

a *buongiorno*, *grazie* and *arrivederci* at the appropriate moments, are always welcomed, as is handshaking, and a polite *piacere* on being introduced to someone. Despite the sartorial style of the young and television presenters, some decorum is expected in religious buildings. Swimwear is definitely not permitted, skimpy shorts and T-shirts frowned upon, though Bermuda shorts and bare shoulders seem to be generally accepted nowadays. Topless sunbathing is still outlawed although the ruling is not enforced.

Language

Apart from the national language, Italian, most Italians involved in the tourist industry also speak English and French. Florentine Italian is considered the best in Italy, hence the proliferation of language schools.

Useful Phrases

Good day • *Buon giorno*
Good evening • *Buona sera*
Hi or Bye • *Ciao*
Goodbye • *Arrivederci*
Please • *Per piacere*
Thanks • *Grazie*
Okay • *D'accordo*
Excuse me • *Mi scusi*
I'm sorry • *Mi dispiace*
How are you? • *Come sta?*
Fine, thanks • *Bene, grazie*
Help • *Aiuto*
I do not feel well • *Non mi sento bene*
Please call a doctor • *Chiami un medico per favore*
What time does it open? • *A che ora apre?*
Where is? • *Dov'è?*
What time is it? • *Che ora è? (or in the afternoon: Che ora sono?)*
Do you speak English? French? • *Parla Inglese? Francese?*
I don't understand • *Non capisco*
Please speak more slowly • *Parli più lentemente per favore*
Open • *Aperto*
Closed • *Chiuso*
How much does this cost? • *Quanto costa questo?*
Too expensive • *Troppo caro*
Bank • *La banca*
ATM • *Il bancomat*
Post office • *L'ufficio postale*
Pharmacy • *La farmacia*
Book store • *La libreria*
Library • *La biblioteca*
Municipality • *Comune*

INDEX OF SIGHTS

GENERAL INDEX

GENERAL INDEX